BERKLEE PRESS

The Songwriter's Workshop

HARMONY

berklee
press

Jimmy Kachulis

Edited by Jonathan Feist

Berklee Media

Vice President: Dave Kusek
Dean of Continuing Education: Debbie Cavalier
Business Manager: Rob Green
Technology Manager: Mike Serio
Marketing Manager, Berkleemusic: Barry Kelly
Senior Graphic Designer: David Ehlers

Berklee Press

Senior Writer/Editor: Jonathan Feist
Senior Writer/Editor: Susan Gedutis Lindsay
Production Manager: Shawn Girsberger
Marketing Manager, Berklee Press: Jennifer D'Angora
Product Marketing Manager: David Goldberg
Production Assistant: Louis O'choa

ISBN 0-634-02661-5

1140 Boylston Street
Boston, MA 02215-3693 USA
(617) 747-2146

Visit Berklee Press Online at
www.berkleepress.com

DISTRIBUTED BY

HAL•LEONARD®
CORPORATION
7777 W. BLUEMOUND RD. P.O. BOX 13819
MILWAUKEE, WISCONSIN 53213

Visit Hal Leonard Online at
www.halleonard.com

Printed in the United States of America

12 11 10 09 08 07 06 05   5 4 3 2 1

CONTENTS

CD TRACKS

Unit IX. Modulation

Play-Along Drum Tracks

Use these play-along drum tracks for each lesson's writing exercises.

PREFACE

This book is designed for songwriters who can play some chords and want to learn how to use them to create songs. It gives a foundation for the melodic tools covered in *The Songwriter's Workshop: Melody* book.

Harmony is one of the essential parts of a modern song. There are two different approaches to the way harmony is used in a song: one from Africa and one from Europe.

The Africans created chord progressions that cycle over and over, with a rhythmic feel or groove. These ideas are covered in units I to V. In this approach, the key's general color and the groove's rhythms reflect the overall mood of the lyric story.

The Europeans created the types of chords (major, minor, and so on) and most of the keys we play. These ideas are introduced in units II and III.

They also created the idea that chords are in a key, and are classified as being "home" or "away from home." This approach emphasizes movement of chords towards the I chord, "home," and the way a chord can color the meaning of an individual word or phrase. These ideas are covered in detail in units IV, and VII to IX.

Modern popular songs combine these two approaches to harmony: the European and the African. Considering both types of influences may help lead you to ideas during your own songwriting process.

ACKNOWLEDGMENTS

Thanks to all of the following:

Debbie Cavalier, Dean of Continuing Education at Berklee, for her initial vision of this series, and her unstinting support through all its various incarnations. From the beginning to the end, her ideas were always crucial to its completion.

Jonathan Feist, at Berklee Press, whose insights into structuring the subject matter and focusing the topics and writing style have contributed immeasurably to this series. The series' success is due in large part to his continual creative input.

Sue Gedutis Lindsay, at Berklee Press, for taking the extra time to read and suggest critical improvements.

Jack Perricone, Chair of the Songwriting Department at Berklee, for his insights into the way songs work. As author of *Melody in Songwriting*, he has inspired countless people to better their writing skills.

Pat Pattison, Professor of Songwriting at Berklee, for starting the whole songwriting program at Berklee, and for his staggering insights into lyric structure and content. His books on lyric writing are an inspiration to scores of people worldwide. Without his dedication and inspiration, none of what we do as songwriting teachers would be possible.

Jon Aldrich, Associate Professor of Songwriting at Berklee, whose encouragement and insights into the writing process have been a continual delight.

Andy Koss, Caroline Gulde, and Matt Pryor, for their wonderful performances and production on the recording, contributing to the success of this project.

All my students—past, present, and future—who gave me their trust as a teacher. If they only knew that I learn much more from them than they ever learned from me.

Most of all, Anne and Maria Terese, for their love and understanding. Without them, none of this would have been possible.

BASICS

To get the most out of this book, you should understand the following musical concepts.

Musical Alphabet

Notes are named for the first seven letters of the alphabet, A to G. They often appear graphically, on a musical staff:

A   B   C   D   E   F   G   A

Below, you can see how the note names relate to the guitar and keyboard. Two octaves (registers) are shown.

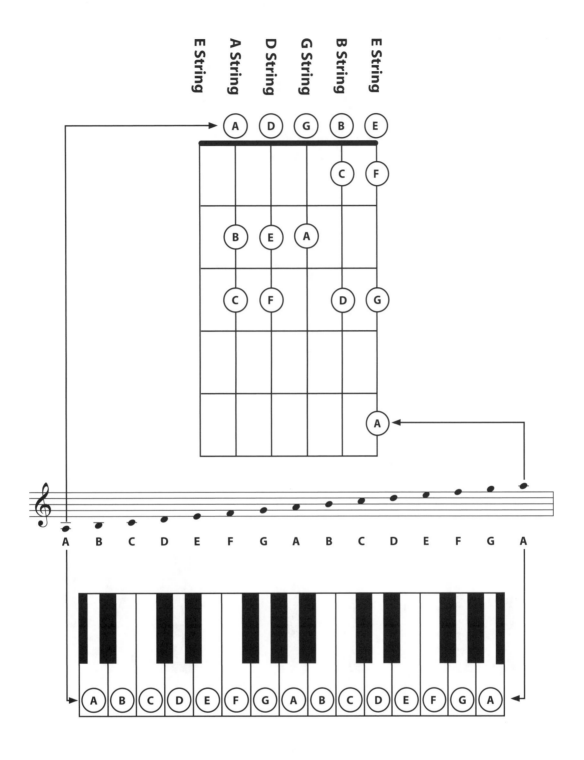

Notes between these basic letters are indicated by *sharps* (♯) or *flats* (♭), depending on the context. These *accidentals* can be cancelled by a *natural* sign (♮). Below, the ties connect different note names for the same pitch. The set of all twelve notes, in an octave, is called the "chromatic scale."

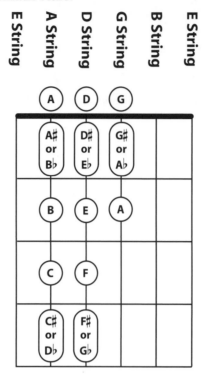

A · A♯ · B♭ · B · C · C♯ · D♭ · D · D♯ · E♭ · E · F · F♯ · G♭ · G · G♯ · A♭ · A

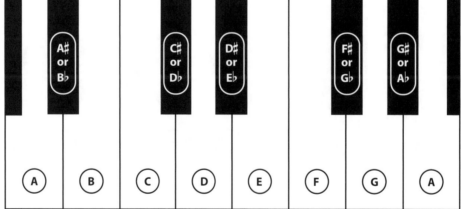

Key Signatures

Key signatures indicate a tune's key and show which notes automatically get sharps or flats. *Accidentals* on the lines and spaces in the key signature affect those notes throughout the tune unless there is a natural sign. Here are the key signatures used in this book.

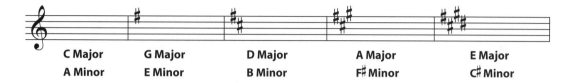

C Major	G Major	D Major	A Major	E Major
A Minor	E Minor	B Minor	F♯ Minor	C♯ Minor

Chords

All chords have three defining characteristics: the *root, type,* and *added notes.*

- *Roots* are the musical letter names (A, B♭, F♯).

- *Types* include major, minor (min), diminished (°) and augmented (+). In this book, we abbreviate minor as "min." You may also see lowercase "m" or a dash (–).

- *Added notes* are any numbers that are in the note name (7, 9, 13).

Chords are named with these three parts, for example:

Amin	A minor has an A *root*, minor *type*, and no added notes.
C	C major has a C root, major type, and no added notes. (In this book, we usually omit the word "major," when used to describe a chord type.)
B♭7	B♭7 has a B♭ root, major type, and a 7 added.
Emin7(9)	Emin7(9) has an E root, minor type, and a 7 and 9 added.

Most of the examples in this book use major and minor chords, with different notes added to them.

Transposition

Transposing means changing the key of a song. This can make it easier to play or easier to sing.

Transposing songs from one key to another is easy:

■ Move all of the chord *roots* the same distance.

■ Keep the type and added notes the same, relative to the new root.

If you have trouble transposing, try using this chart. For example, let's transpose the progression "B♭ Gmin7 Cmin7 F7" to make it easier to play. Begin by choosing the first chord (B♭). Then, follow this procedure:

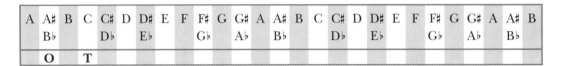

1. Chart the first chord's root. In our progression, the chord roots are the notes B♭, G, C, and F. Locate the first chord's root (B♭) on the chart. The "O" (original) in the chart above shows its location.

2. Locate the target transposition. Let's transpose this B♭ chord to C, so that it will be easier to play. The C chord is marked with a "T" (transposition) in the chart.

3. Count the distance. In this case, C is two spots to the right of B♭. This corresponds to two higher frets on the guitar, two higher keys on the piano, or two higher notes of the chromatic scale.

4. Transpose the other chords. *Move all other chord roots the same distance*—in this case, two spots to the right. They change as follows:

   • B♭ becomes C

   • G becomes A

   • C becomes D

   • F becomes G

5. Return the types and added notes to the chord roots. The transposed progression is much easier to play.

Original Progression:	B♭	Gmin7	Cmin7	F7
Transposed Progression:	C	Amin7	Dmin7	G7

The appendix shows charts of notes and guitar diagrams for many chords in many keys and transpositions.

Now, let's write some songs.

OVERVIEW
The Songwriter's Workshop: Harmony

The Songwriter's Workshop series is designed for songwriters at all levels—from beginners who can't read a note of music to professional songwriters who are looking for new ideas to spice up their work. Each book presents a set of tools for writing songs, with practice exercises. *These tools, examples, and exercises are all based on hit songs.*

This new approach to teaching songwriting is based on using your ear. It makes songwriting easy, fun, and intuitive. There are two main goals. First, you will be able create chord progressions and grooves in any of the five most common key colors. Second, you will be able to use harmony to bring out the meaning of your lyrics.

Learning to use these tools and techniques will have a profound effect on your writing. After completing the lessons, you will be able to:

- Generate original variations of any chord progression you learn.

- Create chord progressions that capture the feeling of a lyric story.

- Create chord progressions that fulfill your audience's expectations—or surprise them.

- Use chord progressions to emphasize your song's title.

- Develop your ideas into complete song sections.

- Compose song sections that work well together, but include enough contrast to keep your ideas sounding fresh.

Do these books. Don't just *read* them. Doing the exercises will help you absorb each tool into your soul, so that you can use the tool to express what you feel. Songwriting is like learning a language. First, you learn the tools of language—words, and sentences that put the words together to express ideas. Then, you learn the tools and techniques of songwriting, and explore songs that use these techniques to express ideas. In this way, you build an "internal library" of ideas, which you can draw upon when you want to articulate what you feel.

Throughout this book, you'll use chord progressions from real hit songs, but will also learn to create your own variations. In using the hits as a starting point, you'll learn to write the way professional songwriters do: borrowing successful elements from various sources, and then reworking them into something new and unique. This approach provides a solid foundation for your new ideas.

Each lesson presents a songwriting tool and then lists songs of different styles that use it. Learn those songs or others like them. Learn from recordings and from fake books. This will build your inner library of songwriting tools.

Though the inspiration for a song may come from your heart, the ability to create a song is a skill. As you hone your songwriting skills, your expressive skills will improve also.

Songwriting Cycle

Songs grow out of four dimensions, as shown below: melody, harmony, form, and lyrics. When you create a song, you will be working with all four aspects, switching between them constantly. Ideas about a chord progression may lead you to a melody, or a lyric may lead to an idea about form.

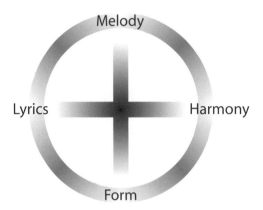

This book is about harmony, and as you perform the exercises, harmony should be in the forefront of your concentration. After this book, your attention to harmony should return to be in balance with the other elements. As this book will enrich your ability to create chord progressions, the other books will enrich your abilities with the other dimensions of songwriting.

Harmony Cycle

Harmony in songwriting includes five dimensions: chords, key, rhythm, lyrics, and melody. Though this book's exercises generally address one dimension at a time, when you write your own songs, you most likely will be working with more than one of them at the same time.

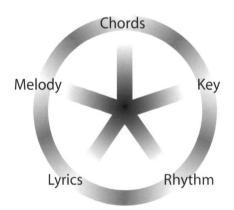

How to Use This Book

Each unit addresses a different type of harmonic tool, with two groups of lessons. The "Ideas" lessons (part A) present tools for creating chords or chord progression ideas. The "Song Sections" lessons (part B) help you develop these ideas into songs or song sections. Each lesson presents a tool, gives examples of hit songs that use the tool, shows how the tool can be used, and then offers a series of exercises. The accompanying CD lets you hear the tool being used in a song. It also provides drum tracks for you to try out the chord progressions and songs you create. Set aside at least half an hour to work on each lesson.

You'll develop the ideas you created in each unit's "Ideas" lessons in the "Song Sections" lessons. I suggest that you use a tape recorder or notate the music. When you practice your ideas and songs, feel free to use your own rhythm tracks. If you play a guitar or keyboard, you can use different chords than the ones used on the recording.

Each lesson will explore ways that you can use the songwriting tools. You may be asked to create a groove, select keys that reflect the overall emotion of the song, or use harmony to emphasize particular lyrics.

Each lesson follows the same two-part format: first, it presents the concept, then it gives you exercises. There are also listening exercises, and as you listen, try to follow the music notation. Since this series is based on using your ear, you don't need the notation to learn the tools, but do watch the notation as you listen. It's the easiest way to learn to read music. Reading the lyrics will help you keep your place.

After you listen, play along with each track, to train your ear and understand the tool. After the audio example is a discussion of the tool's musical effect, its effect on the lyrics' emotional content, and its common uses.

Exercises

The exercises in each lesson are presented in four levels. *Do at least one level in each lesson.* Later, go through the book again and try a different level. The levels are designed for songwriters at many levels of experience, and as you grow as a songwriter, you will use this book in different ways. Here are the levels of exercises:

Practice exercises delve into the tool in its simplest form. They are especially suitable for beginning songwriters. At this level, you will learn the tool by changing one aspect of the given example.

Rewrite the Hits exercises bring you into real-world examples of how songs are written by professionals. You will choose a song you know that uses the tool, and then you will rewrite it. *This is the most common way that professionals write songs!* We take a small idea from an existing song we love, or in the style we are trying to imitate, and use it as a jumping-off point for our own unique song.

Create Your Own Melody exercises are for writers who can create melodies. Songwriters sometimes work together, with one writer focusing on melody and the other on harmony. These exercises will help you practice adding melodies onto chord progressions studied in the lesson.

Write a Song exercises give more experienced songwriters the opportunity to create full songs based on the tool being discussed. Though the lessons are based on simple scales and chords, you can practice using the tools with more complex materials. At this level, you create complete songs with the lesson's tool, and also get some tips for creating contrasting song sections.

Do whatever level inspires you. The level you choose may depend on your skill level, your mood, or how much time you have. The important part is that you put the tools into practice as soon as you learn them. Whenever writer's block strikes, flip through the book for some quick ideas.

As you learn these tools of harmony, think about what the song's lyric story might be about, and how the tools can support the lyric. The goal of harmony is ultimately to strengthen the emotional impact of your song. Understanding how these tools can help to support your lyrics will make the tools much more useful to you.

Every songwriter is unique, and you will come to use these tools of harmony in your own way. Eventually, you will use them without thinking about them, and just write by ear.

Good luck!

Jimmy Kachulis
Professor
Berklee College of Music

UNIT I
Generating a Groove

We begin the exploration of harmony in songwriting with a discussion of grooves. Rhythmically speaking, a groove is made up of the tempo, feel, rhythmic level, and rhythmic motives. These rhythmic elements combine with chords to reflect the meaning of the lyric story.

Some songwriters begin their creative process by writing the groove. Then, they create lyrics that reflect the emotion of the groove. Alternatively, some create the lyric story first, and then find a groove to reflect the lyric emotion. *Either approach is fine, as long as the lyric story and the feeling of the music are intimately connected.*

A. Parts of a Groove

In part A, we will look at how to write grooves. Look at the elements of a song in this order, when developing a groove:

1. **Tempo** is the speed of the song. What speed brings out the emotional meaning of the lyric story? Fast? Medium? Slow? Each tempo has its own feeling.

2. **Feel** is the style that the song is in. What style would reflect the song's story? Rock? R&B? Country? Rap? Each style also has its own feeling.

3. **Rhythmic level** refers to the type of rhythms that are in the groove. Does it use whole notes? Half notes? Quarter notes? Eighth notes? Sixteenth notes? Triplets?

4. **Rhythmic idea** (also called "rhythmic motive") is a short, distinctive pattern that propels the song forward. Rhythm motives are usually developed to distinguish each song section.

LESSON 1
Creating a Groove

In this lesson, we will look at four aspects of grooves: tempo, feel, rhythmic level, and rhythmic idea.

Most hit songs are based on grooves. The groove can be as important as the melody or harmony, especially in styles such as funk.

Reuse Grooves

One of the best ways to start writing songs is to use grooves from songs you know. Use the same groove, but change the chords.

Listen

Listen to the following three grooves, based on a C major chord. Notice the medium tempo and rock feel. Each groove demonstrates a different rhythmic level.

> Groove 1 uses whole, half, and quarter notes.
> Groove 2 uses eighth and quarter notes.
> Groove 3 uses sixteenth notes.

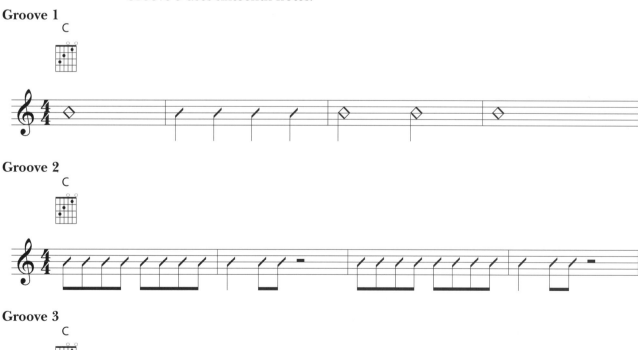

Listen again, and play a C chord along with each groove's rhythmic idea. Notice that the rhythmic motives are all different lengths (four measures, two measures, and one measure).

Also notice how a single chord can yield many different ideas, when used in different grooves. As you learn more about chords, be sure to try them in many different types of grooves.

Writing Exercises

 to Complete at least one of these exercises. Play and practice your groove along with one of the drum tracks, or create your own rhythm groove.

■ Practice

Create a groove on any chord. Choose a tempo, feel, and rhythmic level, and create a rhythmic idea. What emotion are you trying to communicate?

■ Rewrite the Hits

Create a groove by combining a chord progression and a rhythmic motive from two different songs. What emotion does this groove suggest?

■ Create Your Own Melody

Create a groove by combining a chord progression and a rhythmic motive from two different songs. Then create your own melodic idea over the chord progression. What emotion does this combination of groove and melody suggest?

■ Write a Song

Create a groove by combining a chord progression and a rhythmic motive from two different songs. Then create your own melodic idea with lyrics over the chord progression. What emotion does this song suggest?

What's the Story?

What do you think the lyric story will be about? What will be the main emotion of your song?

As you do the exercises in this book, always ask yourself these questions. These tools all strengthen the emotional impact of your song, and understanding how will make them much more useful to you.

B. Building a Song Section

In part B, we will use different development tools to build song sections.

LESSON 2
Developing a Groove

Once you choose the tempo, feel, rhythmic level, and rhythmic motive for your song, you can use different tools to develop it into a song section (verse, chorus, bridge, etc.). Most hit songs develop sections out of grooves in one of three ways.

1. Exact repetition. The groove's rhythmic idea is repeated exactly.

2. Varied repetition. The rhythmic idea is repeated with something changed.

3. Adding another motive. A new rhythmic idea is combined or alternated with the original one.

Listen

Listen to the following example, based on the rhythmic ideas from lesson 1. Notice how the ideas develop.

1. Exact Repetition

2. Varied Repetition

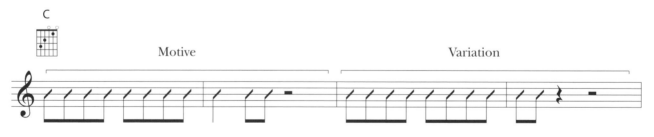

3. Added Motive

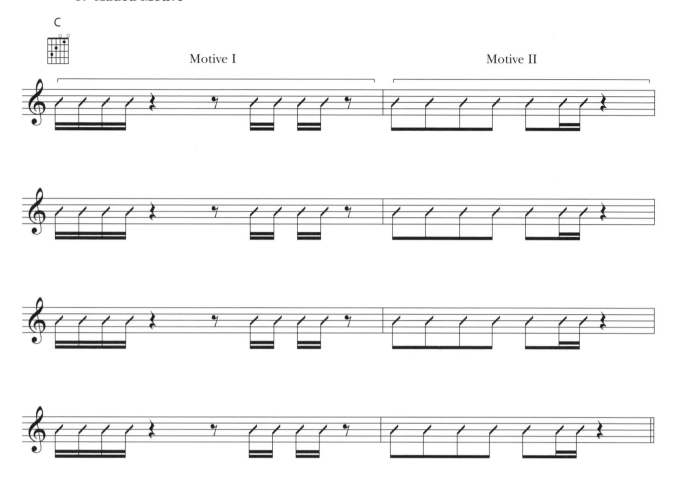

Listen again, and play a C chord along with the recording. Notice that each example develops its rhythmic idea into an 8-measure song section. Developing your song sections from one or two rhythmic ideas helps to give the entire song a distinctive personality.

Writing Exercises

Complete at least one of these exercises. Play and practice your groove along with one of the drum tracks, or create your own rhythm groove.

■ Practice

Using the rhythmic idea you created in the previous lesson, create three sections of eight measures each.

Section 1. Use exact repetition.
Section 2. Use varied repetition.
Section 3. Use two different motives.

■ Rewrite the Hits

Complete the "Practice" exercise above using a rhythmic idea from a hit song.

■ Create Your Own Melody

Complete either the "Practice" or "Rewrite the Hits" exercise above. Then create your own melody on top of this groove.

■ Write a Song

Complete the "Create Your Own Melody" above. Then create your own lyrics to go along with that melody.

UNIT II
Chord Colors and Lyric Stories

In part A of this unit, you'll learn the four most common chord "colors" used in songwriting and their effect on lyrics. You'll also learn how to combine these colors with the rhythmic ideas you learned in unit I to create a unique groove for every song.

Songwriting is like painting. You need to choose the chord color that best expresses the lyric's emotion. What does a painting express if it uses mostly blue? What about red? Picasso painted in shades of blue and red at different periods of his life. In music, one of our main musical styles is even called "blues," and it is characterized by a pattern of chords and colors.

As songwriters, we try to develop our awareness of musical colors. It can be helpful to associate actual colors with sounds and feelings, as a way of getting to know our chords more intimately so that we use them more effectively. Here are some ideas for how to develop this awareness.

■ Look at a color. Then find that color on your instrument, using notes to reflect the same feeling that color gives you.

■ Play a chord and describe the color it suggests to you.

■ Describe an emotion using some of the chords you learn in this unit.

■ Play a chord and describe the emotion it conveys to you.

In part B, you'll develop a chord's basic color by adding notes. You will then use these chord variations to create grooves.

A. Four Chord Colors

Once you have your rhythmic groove, the next step is to choose chords. Combining the right chord colors into your rhythmic grooves will help you to express the emotion of the lyric story.

LESSON 3
Major Chord Color

The first chord color is *major*. For most people, "major" reflects feelings that are generally happy and optimistic. As you play the examples in these lessons, always be aware of the emotions they bring up for you.

Hit songs that have grooves on a major chord include "Walk This Way" [C], "Emotional Rescue" [B♭], "Gimme Shelter" [D♭], and many others.

Keys of Hits

Brackets [ ] following song titles show the original key used on the original recordings.

Major chords have three notes: the *root, major third*, and *fifth*. For example, the C major chord has these three notes:

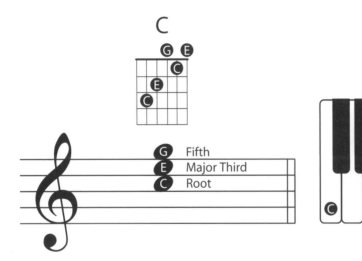

Listen

Listen to the C major chord, first strummed (all notes at once) and then played as an *arpeggio* (one note at a time). Then, listen to the groove.

Listen again, and play along with the track. The major third (E) is the note that gives the chord its "major," happy, positive sound. Notice that the 1-measure motive is repeated exactly (see lesson 2).

What do you think the lyric story of this song will be about? What will be the main emotion?

Borrowing and Combining

In this example, I started my songwriting process by taking the chords from "Walk This Way" and the groove from "Taxman." This is an important songwriting technique: other songs can be good sources for ideas. Though these two songs were the basis for this example, it does not really sound exactly like either one. It is something new.

Writing Exercises

Complete at least one of these exercises. Play and practice it along with one of the drum tracks, or create your own rhythm groove. Use any of the rhythmic tools from unit I to generate your grooves. Transpose the chords, if you need to.

■ Practice

Create a 1-measure major-chord groove on a C major chord.

■ Rewrite the Hits

Choose a major-chord groove from any song you know (or one listed in this lesson). Create a new groove on that chord to transform it into an original song.

■ Create Your Own Melody

Complete the "Practice" or "Rewrite the Hits" exercise above. Create your own melody on top of this groove.

■ Write a Song

Create a song section, with melody and lyrics, over a major-chord groove.

LESSON 4
Minor Chord Color

The second chord color is *minor*. For most people, minor reflects sad or introspective feelings.

Hit songs that have grooves on a minor chord include "I'm a Man" [Cmin], "I'm Just a Singer in a Rock and Roll Band" [Amin], "Let It Ride" [F♯min], "Saturday Night Special" [Gmin], "Best Things in Life Are Free" [F♯min], "Fire" [Dmin], "Spanish Castle Magic" [C♯min], "You Give Love a Bad Name" [Cmin], and many others.

Minor chords have three notes: the root, *minor* third, and fifth. For example, the A minor chord has these three notes:

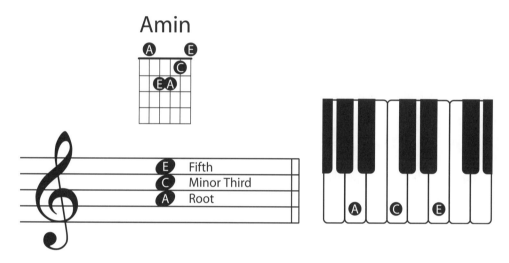

Listen

Listen to the A minor chord strummed and then played as an arpeggio. Then listen to the groove.

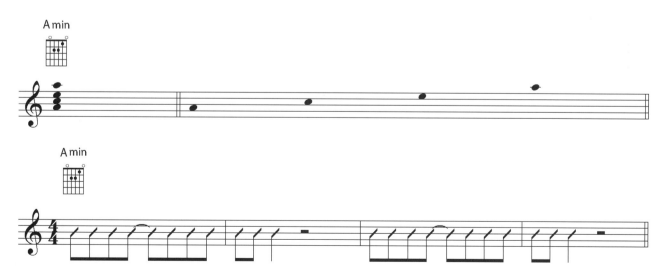

Listen again, and play along with the track. The minor third (C) is the note that gives the chord its "sad," somber sound. Notice that the motive is two measures long.

What do you think the lyric story of this song will be about? What will be the main emotion?

Writing Exercises

Complete at least one of these exercises. Play and practice it along with one of the drum tracks, or create your own rhythm groove. Use any of the rhythmic tools from unit I to generate your grooves. Transpose the chords, if you need to.

■ Practice

Create a 1-measure minor-chord groove on an A minor chord.

■ Rewrite the Hits

Choose a minor-chord groove from any song you know (or one listed in this lesson). Create a new groove on that chord to transform it into an original song.

■ Create Your Own Melody

Complete the "Practice" or "Rewrite the Hits" exercise above. Create your own melody on top of this groove.

■ Write a Song

Create a song section, with melody and lyrics, over a minor-chord groove.

LESSON 5
Power Chord Color

The third chord color is the *power chord*. For most people it reflects feelings that are strong, assertive, even aggressive. At a slow tempo, it can also sound mysterious.

Hit songs that have grooves on a power chord include "I Love Rock and Roll" [E5], "Bad Medicine" [E5], "Barracuda" [E5], and many others.

Power chords have two notes: the root and fifth. Often, the root is doubled, up an octave.

For example, the E power chord (E5) has these two notes (shown with the doubled octave):

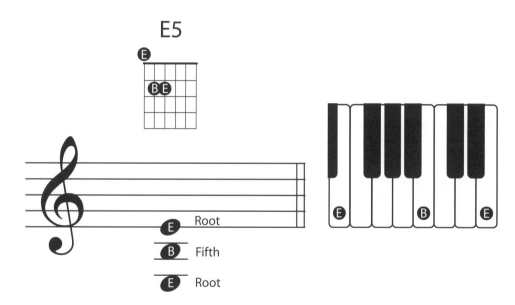

Listen

Listen to the E power chord strummed and then played as an arpeggio. Then listen to the groove.

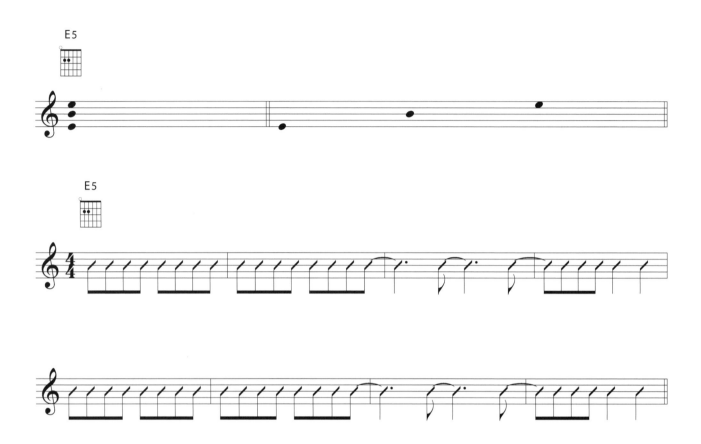

Listen again, and play along with the track. The unique sound of the power chord comes from not having any third at all. Notice that the motive comes from combining two different 2-measure figures.

What do you think the lyric story of the song will be about? What will be the main emotion?

Writing Exercises

Complete at least one of these exercises. Play and practice it along with one of the drum tracks, or create your own rhythm groove. Use any of the rhythmic tools from unit I to generate your grooves. Transpose the chords, if you need to.

■ Practice

Create a 1-measure groove on an E5 power chord.

■ Rewrite the Hits

Choose a power-chord groove from any song you know (or one listed in this lesson). Create a new groove on that chord to transform it into an original song.

■ Create Your Own Melody

Complete the "Practice" or "Rewrite the Hits" exercise above. Create your own melody on top of this groove.

■ Write a Song

Create a song section, with melody and lyrics, over a power-chord groove.

LESSON 6
Seventh Chord Color

The fourth chord color is the *seventh chord*. For most people, it reflects feelings that are bluesy, funky, even sexy.

Hit songs that have grooves on a seventh chord include "The Beat Goes On" [C7], "Dancin' in the Street" [E7], "Goin' to a Go-Go" [G7], "Day Tripper" [E7], "Proud Mary" [G7], "Last Child" [Eb7], "Taxman" [D7], and many others.

Seventh chords have four notes: the root, major third, fifth, and seventh.

For example, the G7 has these four notes:

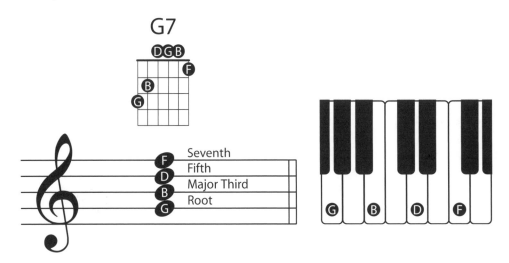

Listen

Listen to the G7 chord strummed and then played as an arpeggio. Then, listen to the groove.

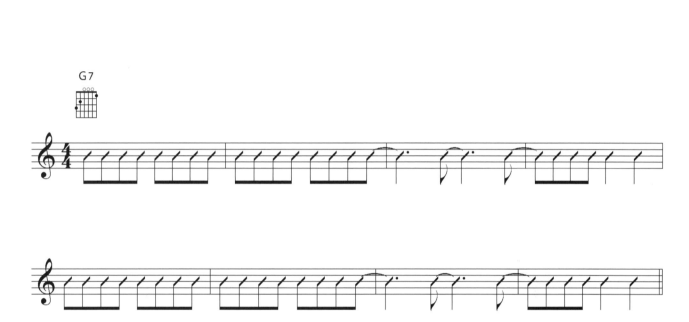

Listen again, and play along with the track. The bluesy sound of this chord comes from the seventh that's added onto a major chord. Notice the groove is four variations on an original 1-measure motive.

What do you think the lyric story of the song will be about? What will be the main emotion?

Writing Exercises

Complete at least one of these exercises. Play and practice it along with one of the drum tracks, or create your own rhythm groove. Use any of the rhythmic tools from unit I to generate your grooves. Transpose the chords, if you need to.

■ Practice

Create a 1-measure seventh-chord groove on a G7 chord.

■ Rewrite the Hits

Choose a seventh-chord groove from any song you know (or one listed in this lesson). Create a new groove on that chord to transform it into an original song.

■ Create Your Own Melody

Complete the "Practice" or "Rewrite the Hits" exercise above. Create your own melody on top of this groove.

■ Write a Song

Create a song section, with melody and lyrics, over a seventh-chord groove.

B. Varying Chord Colors

Adding notes to your basic chords will give new and subtle colors to your grooves. You can also create a groove using two or more versions of the same basic chord color, by skillfully adding notes.

LESSON 7
Variations of Chord Colors

The chord families in part A are *general* colors. You can vary a chord's basic color subtly by adding or replacing notes. Varying chord colors like this can be used in all four chord colors, in all styles of music.

Hit songs using 1-chord grooves with notes added include "Fame" [G9], "Shining Star" [E7($\sharp$9)], and many others.

Listen

 Listen to the Dmin chord followed by the Dmin7 chord, as shown in the next example. Notice that the Dmin7 adds one note, the seventh, to the Dmin.

Added Note

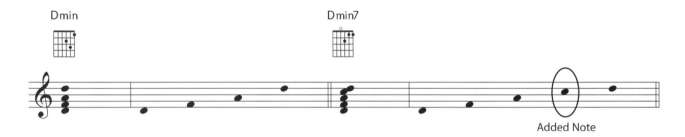

Listen again, and play along. Notice that the added seventh, C, gives a little different color without changing the basic D minor color.

 Next, listen to the A chord, followed by the Asus2 chord. Notice that the sus2 note, B, replaces the third, C-sharp, but doesn't change the overall A major color.

Replaced Note

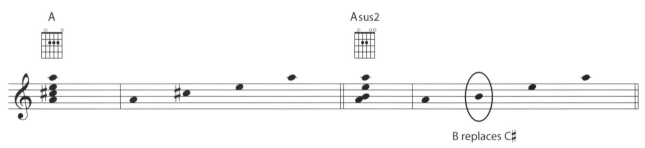

Here are some of the common ways that you can vary chords, by adding and changing notes of the four basic chord colors. The basic chord color and its variations are together called a *chord family*.

Basic Color	Add	Replace a Note and Create:
Major	6, Maj7, Maj9, add2	sus2, sus4
Minor	6, min7, min9, min11, add2	minor sus4
Power	sus2	—
Seventh	9, 13, or ♯9	6, 7sus4, 11

■ Practice

Practice these chords by alternating between the basic chord and each variation.

Listen to this groove, which is based on an A13 chord.

Listen again, and play along. Notice how the bluesy emotion in the lyrics is reflected in the bluesy color of the A13 chord. Also notice the 2-measure rhythmic motive.

Writing Exercises

Complete at least one of these exercises. Play and practice it along with one of the drum tracks, or create your own rhythm groove. Use any of the rhythmic tools from unit I to generate your grooves. Transpose the chords, if you need to.

■ Practice

Choose a 1-chord groove you created in part A of this unit, and change the chord color by adding or replacing notes.

■ Rewrite the Hits

Choose a 1-chord groove from a song you know (or one listed in this lesson). Change the chord color by adding or replacing notes.

■ Create Your Own Melody

Complete the "Practice" or "Rewrite the Hits" exercise above. Create your own melody on top of this groove.

■ Write a Song

Create a song section, with melody and lyrics, by adding or replacing notes in a 1-chord groove.

LESSON 8
Alternating Variations

Alternating between two variations of a chord color is another way to expand on a 1-chord groove.

Hit songs alternating between two variations of a single chord color include "Get Back" [A],"Cold as Ice" [Emin], "Drive" [B], most Chuck Berry songs, and many others.

Notice the different versions of the chords achieved by adding or replacing notes in the basic chord. Also notice how these variations help keep the 1-chord groove interesting.

In the style of "Get Back"

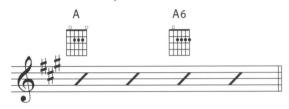

In the style of "Drive"

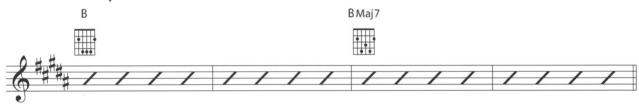

In the style of "Cold as Ice"

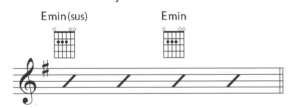

In the style of "Sweet Emotion"

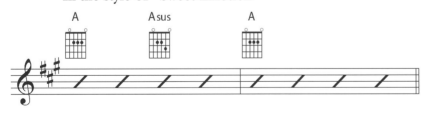

Listen

10 Listen to this progression, which uses two versions of an A minor chord: Amin and Amin(sus). Also, notice that this groove combines two rhythmic motives.

Groove

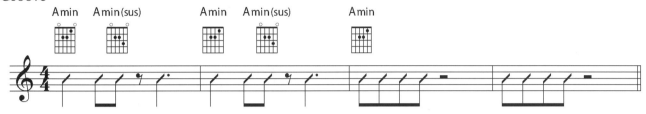

Chorus

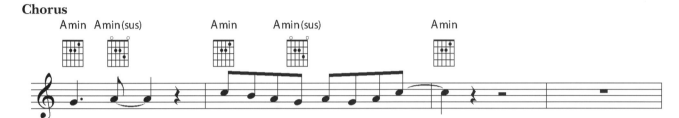

Dark - ness_____   Com - in' to the edge of our town_____

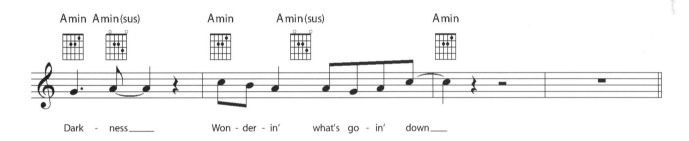

Dark - ness_____   Won - der - in'   what's go - in'   down_____

Listen again, and play along with the recording. Notice how the A minor color reflects the ominous quality of the lyric.

Writing Exercises

Complete at least one of these exercises. Play and practice it along with one of the drum tracks, or create your own rhythm groove. Use any of the rhythmic tools from unit I to generate your grooves. Transpose the chords, if you need to.

■ Practice

Choose one of the 1-chord grooves you created in part A of this unit. Create different variations of the basic chord color. Create a groove by alternating different variations.

■ Rewrite the Hits

Choose a 1-chord groove from a song you know (or one listed in this lesson). Create different variations of the basic chord color. Create a groove by alternating the different variations.

■ Create Your Own Melody

Complete the "Practice" or "Rewrite the Hits" exercise above. Create your own melody on top of this groove.

■ Write a Song

Create a song section, with melody and lyrics, by using different versions of one chord color.

UNIT III
Colors of Keys

In unit II, you learned how to create grooves using just one chord and its variations. Those grooves were actually in a *key*. In this unit, you'll learn about keys, and the scale and chords in a key. The appendix charts all scales and chords for all key colors, in all transpositions.

Keys

A *key* is a set of notes that gravitates, or pulls, towards one note, called the *tonic*. The tonic note gives the key its name and its center. For instance, C is the tonic of the key of C major.

In this unit, we will discuss the most common key colors used in popular music styles: major, minor, Mixolydian, Dorian, and blues.

Most common keys have seven notes. For instance, the key of C major has these seven notes (with a repeated octave, at the end):

On each note, a basic chord can be built with the scale note as the chord *root*, and other scale notes superimposed on top of it, like this:

A key's basic chords are built by stacking *alternate* scale notes above the root, skipping every other note. Using this process, the seven notes in C major can be used to create these basic chords:

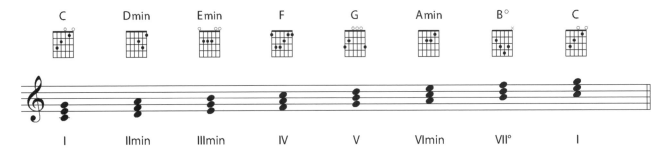

We can reference chords by using Roman numerals based on their scale positions. For instance, in C major, the C chord is described as the "one" chord (I), D minor is the "two" chord (II), and so on. When analyzing chords, Roman numerals are written below the staff.

A. Five Common Key Colors

In unit II, you created song sections using just a single chord. Now, you'll begin learning how to use the other chords in the key. Once you can do this in a major scale, you'll be able to do it in the other common key colors. Later, you'll learn how to use chords from outside the song's key.

Most popular songs are in one of five *key colors*. A key's color is like an expanded color of the I chord. The key has the I chord's basic color, but other dimensions of that color are added to it, coming from additional notes and chords implied by the basic chord.

There are two approaches to using these chords in songs:

■ Progressions that cycle over and over (see units III to VI)

■ Progressions that move away from and then back toward "home" (the tonic, or "I chord;" see units VII to IX)

Once you learn each of these approaches, you will be able to combine them— as great songwriters do—to create songs that express a wide variety of emotions.

Chord Charts

Remember, the appendix includes charts showing the notes and guitar diagrams for the basic chords of the five key colors, in all twelve transpositions.

LESSON 9
Major Key Color

Major is the most common key color. Major keys are like expanded and enriched major chords (see lesson 3). In the key, the tonic major chord is in a relationship with other chords in that key, and they all contribute to the key's overall color and characteristics.

Hit songs in major keys include "Just the Way You Are" [D], "Endless Love" [B♭], "I Want to Hold Your Hand" [G], "Help Me Make It through the Night" [C], "Gone Country" [C], and many others.

Listen

Diatonic Major

Major keys have seven notes and seven chords. Listen to the notes and chords of C major:

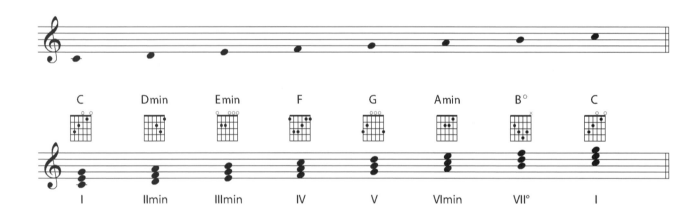

When a note or a chord is in a key, it's said to be *diatonic*. Major keys include diatonic major, minor, and diminished chords, as shown above. You can use all of these chord colors to enrich the way you set the lyric story.

Important Diatonic Chords in Major

In major keys, three families of chords are most important: the tonic, dominant, and subdominant chords.

Tonic Chord (I). The I chord is the most important chord in any key—major or otherwise. It's like being "home," where the listener has a "resolved" feeling. Returning to the tonic is an important way to reflect a resolved feeling in your lyric. In C major, the tonic chord is C.

Dominant Chord (V). The V chord builds tension, and gives the key its strongest unresolved feeling. This sense of tension or lack of resolution in your harmonies helps to reinforce those feelings in your lyrics. This tension is resolved, harmonically, by moving from the dominant to the tonic (V to I). In C major, the dominant chord is G.

Subdominant Chord (IV). The IV chord is more stable than the dominant, but less stable than the tonic. One common way to use the subdominant in grooves is to add harmonic motion by alternating it with the tonic (I/IV/I/IV/I). In C major, the subdominant chord is F.

Using Diatonic Chords: Alternating with the Tonic

Alternating between the tonic chord and another diatonic chord is one of the simplest and most effective types of chord progression. One common alternating-chord progression is I to IV.

All of the following hit songs are based on the I to IV progression: "Imagine," "Baby I Need Your Lovin'," "My Girl," "Shakin' the Tree," "Tonight's the Night," "Sing a Song," "Kiss You All Over," "In Your Eyes," "You Can't Always Get What You Want," "Baby You're a Rich Man," "Walk On," "You Sexy Thing," "Roll on Down the Highway," "Hey, Hey, Hey," "The Way You Do the Things You Do," "ABC," "King of Pain," "Ain't Too Proud to Beg," "Satisfaction," "Tin Man," "Rain," "Gimme Some Lovin'," "Forever Young," "Sweet Emotion," and many others.

Listen to this "I IV" progression in C major.

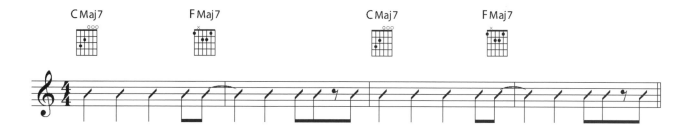

Listen again, and play along with the recording. Although this progression uses the IV chord (FMaj7), it still sounds like it's in the key of C. The subdominant acts like a subtle coloring of the C chord.

Notice that the major sevenths added to the chords give the song a wistful quality.

Writing Exercises

Complete at least one of these exercises. Play and practice it along with one of the drum tracks, or create your own rhythm groove. Use any of the rhythmic tools from unit I to generate your grooves. Transpose the exercises to any major key.

■ Practice

Create a major-key groove on the progression "I IV."

■ Rewrite the Hits

Choose a major-key 2-chord progression from a song you know (or one mentioned in this lesson). Create your own groove to transform it into something new.

■ Create Your Own Melody

Complete the "Practice" or "Rewrite the Hits" exercise above. Create your own melody on top of this groove.

■ Write a Song

Create a song section, with melody and lyrics, using a 2-chord progression in a major key.

LESSON 10
Minor Key Color

Minor is the next most common key color, after major. Minor keys are like expanded versions of minor chords, "colored" with some other chords.

Hit songs in a minor key include "King of Pain" [Bmin], "We Are the Champions" [Cmin], "Walking on the Moon" [Dmin], "Ohio" [Amin], "Where Have All the Cowboys Gone?" [F#min], "Wrapped around Your Finger" [Amin], and many others.

Listen

Listen to the notes and chords of A minor:

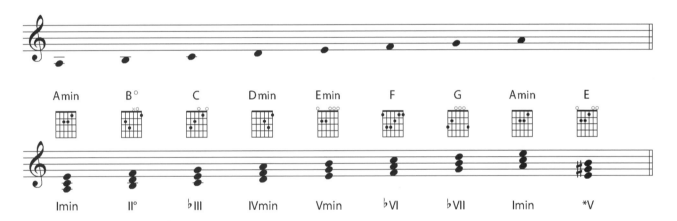

Possible substitution: V for Vmin

Some Roman numerals have a flat symbol (♭) in front of the numeral. This clarifies that the chord is in a minor key, for instance, "flat 6" (♭VI), "flat 7" (♭VII), etc.

The two most important chords in minor are the tonic and the dominant.

Tonic chord. The Imin chord is the most important chord in minor. Although it's also "home," remember that the whole color of this chord, minor, permeates the entire lyric. In the key of A minor, the tonic chord is A minor.

Dominant chords. The minor key has several dominant-type chords that build tension. The Vmin chord and the ♭VII chord are the two most common ones. In A minor, the dominant-type chords are Emin, G, and E.

V in Minor

You can change the color of the Vmin chord to V major, which builds even more tension.

Grooves built by alternating between two chords are common in minor keys, just as in major. One of the most common such progressions is "Imin♭VII" and its variations.

Listen to this A minor progression of "Imin(sus4) to ♭VII."

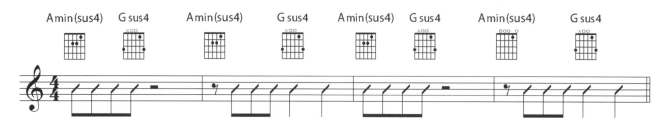

Listen again, and play along with this example. Notice that even though it uses a G major chord (Gsus4), the progression still has a minor feel to it. Also notice that the added notes give the groove a little bit of a jazz feel.

Always try adding notes to the basic chord colors. These will expand your harmonic palette, and will help you to express more subtle emotional colors in your lyrics.

Writing Exercises

Complete at least one of these exercises. Play and practice it along with one of the drum tracks, or create your own rhythm groove. Use any of the rhythmic tools from unit I to generate your grooves. Transpose the exercises to any minor key.

■ Practice

Create a minor-key groove on the progression "Imin♭VII."

■ Rewrite the Hits

Choose a minor-key 2-chord progression from a song you know (or one mentioned in this lesson). Create your own groove to transform it into something new.

■ Create Your Own Melody

Complete the "Practice" or "Rewrite the Hits" exercise above. Create your own melody on top of this groove.

■ Write a Song

Create a song section, with melody and lyrics, using a 2-chord progression in a minor key.

LESSON 11
Mixolydian Key Color

The Mixolydian color is especially common in rock and r&b styles. You can hear it as an outgrowth of the seventh chord, "colored" with other chords.

Hit songs in Mixolydian include "Paperback Writer" [G Mixolydian], "Manic Depression" [A Mixolydian], "Fire" [D Mixolydian], "Reelin' in the Years" [A Mixolydian], "Only You Know and I Know" [E♭ Mixolydian], "Tears of a Clown" [D♭ Mixolydian], "Don't Stop 'til You Get Enough" [B Mixolydian], "Norwegian Wood" [E Mixolydian], "Saturday Night's Alright" [G Mixolydian and C Mixolydian], "My Generation" [F Mixolydian], "Centerfold" [G Mixolydian], "Boogie Fever" [F Mixolydian], "Hollywood Nights" [E Mixolydian], and many others.

Listen

Listen to the notes and chords of G Mixolydian.

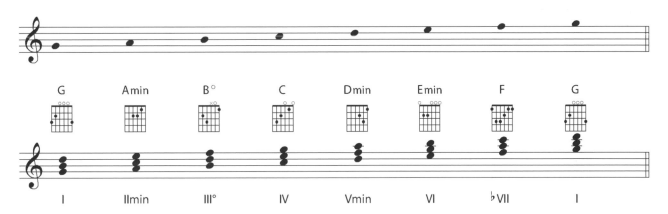

Notice that G Mixolydian sounds like G major with one note changed: the seventh note, F, is flatted. Compare G Mixolydian to G major (see the appendix), and you'll notice that the F is sharp in G major and natural in G Mixolydian.

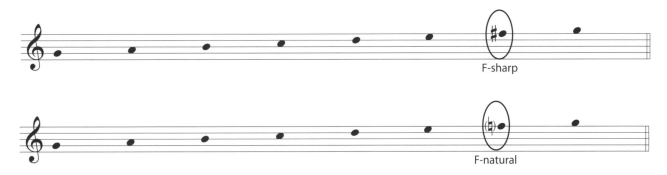

An easy way to think of Mixolydian is as a major key with a flat 7.

Important Mixolydian Chords

The most important chords in Mixolydian are based on the tonic and flat 7.

Tonic Chord. The I chord gives the main color to the Mixolydian key. In G Mixolydian, the tonic chord is G.

Chord Using a Lowered Seventh. Chords that have the lowered 7— usually the ♭VII, less often the Vmin—give Mixolydian its unique color. In G Mixolydian, the lowered 7 is F-natural, and the chords are F and Dmin.

 Listen to this "I ♭VII" progression in G Mixolydian.

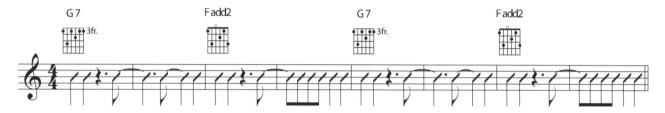

Listen again, and play along with this example. Notice that the F chord, when used in a progression with the G7, emphasizes the Mixolydian sound.

Writing Exercises

 Complete at least one of these exercises. Play and practice it along with one of the drum tracks, or create your own rhythm groove. Use any of the rhythmic tools from unit I to generate your grooves. Transpose the exercises to any Mixolydian key.

■ Practice

Create a Mixolydian key groove on the progression "I ♭VII."

■ Rewrite the Hits

Choose a Mixolydian 2-chord progression from a song you know (or one mentioned in this lesson). Create your own groove to transform it into something new.

■ Create Your Own Melody

Complete the "Practice" or "Rewrite the Hits" exercise above. Create your own melody on top of this groove.

■ Write a Song

Create a song section, with melody and lyrics, using a 2-chord progression in a Mixolydian key.

LESSON 12
Dorian Key Color

The Dorian color is another common key used in rock and r&b styles. Like the minor key, you can hear Dorian as an outgrowth of the minor chord.

Hit songs in a Dorian key include "Evil Ways" [A Dorian], "I Wish" [E♭ Dorian], "Lowdown" [F Dorian], "Foxy Lady" [F♯ Dorian], "Owner of a Lonely Heart" [A Dorian], "Moondance" [A Dorian], "Billie Jean" [F♯ Dorian], and many others.

Listen

Listen to the notes and chords in D Dorian:

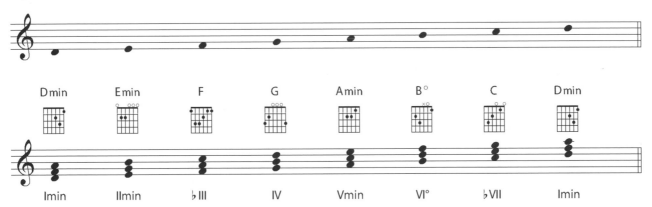

Notice that D Dorian sounds like D minor, with one note changed: the sixth, B, is not flatted, in Dorian. Compare D Dorian to D Minor, and notice that B is flat in D minor and natural in Dorian.

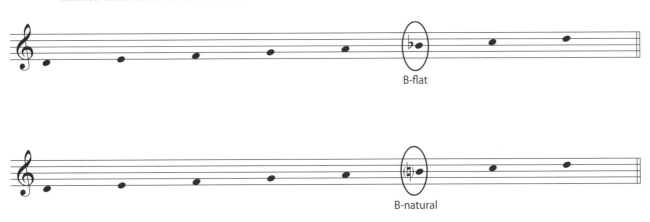

An easy way to think of Dorian is as a minor key with a raised sixth.

Important Chords

The most important chords in Dorian are the tonic and chords that include the raised sixth.

Tonic Chord. The Imin chord gives the main color to the Dorian key. In D Dorian, the tonic chord is Dmin.

Chords Using a Raised Sixth. Usually the IV major or IV7, and less often the IImin. Chords that have the raised sixth—usually the IV major or IV7—give Dorian its special color. In D Dorian, the raised sixth is B-natural, and the chords are G7 and Emin.

 Listen to this "Imin IV" chord progression used in "Lowdown," "I Wish," "Black Water," "It's Too Late," "Dance, Dance, Dance," and "I'm Alright." Here, it is set in E Dorian.

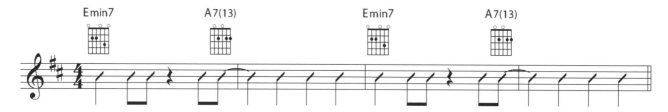

Listen again, and play along with this example. Notice that the A7(13) chord brings out the special color of E Dorian.

Writing Exercises

 Complete at least one of these exercises. Play and practice it along with one of the drum tracks, or create your own rhythm groove. Use any of the rhythmic tools from unit I to generate your grooves. Transpose the exercises to any Dorian key.

■ Practice

Create a Dorian key groove on the progression "Imin IV" or "Imin IV7."

■ Rewrite the Hits

Choose a Dorian 2-chord progression from a song you know (or one mentioned in this lesson). Create your own groove to transform it into something new.

■ Create Your Own Melody

Complete the "Practice" or "Rewrite the Hits" exercise above. Create your own melody on top of this groove.

■ Write a Song

Create a song section, with melody and lyrics, using a 2-chord progression in a Dorian key.

LESSON 13
Blues Key Color

The blues key color is very common, and it has influenced all styles of popular music. It mixes the major and minor key colors in a unique way. Blues is usually in major. Like Mixolydian, you can hear it as an enriched version of the seventh chord, colored with other chords.

Hit songs in a blues key include "Rock Me" [C blues], "Jumpin' Jack Flash" [B♭ blues], "Higher Ground" [E♭ blues], "Purple Haze" [E blues], "I Can See for Miles" [E blues], "After Midnight" [C blues], "She's a Woman" [A blues], "Long Cool Woman in a Black Dress" [E blues], "Pink Cadillac" [E blues], "Give Me One Reason" [G blues], and many others.

The blues has African roots. Originally, it had no chords—just someone playing one note in the bass and singing the different blues scales over that one note. After a while, blues songwriters found that they could combine these notes together to form blues-style chords.

The best way to think of blues harmony is to learn the most common blues chords used in a major blues key.

Listen

Listen to the notes and chords of the major and minor blues keys. The two blues key colors are mixed together to create a rich group of chord colors. This mixture makes the blues unique—different from the others you have learned.

C Major Blues

C Minor Blues

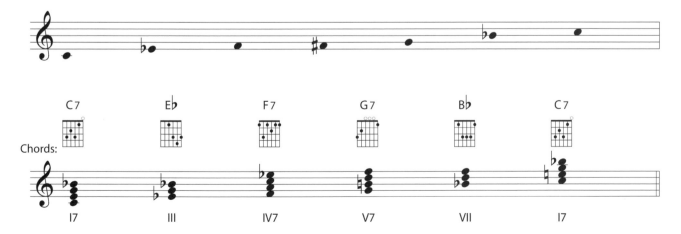

Notice that the C blues key sounds like C major with some other notes mixed in. Blues chords are different from major key chords in a few ways:

1. Compare the C blues chords with the C major chords. The CMaj7 and FMaj7 chords of major are now C7 and F7 in blues. The added seventh on each chord, which is optional in all the other scales, is usually included in blues keys, giving a song a blues color.

2. Compare the C blues scale with the C minor scale. Notice that the ♭III chord and the ♭VII chord in the blues scale are actually *chords from the minor scale that are mixed into the major blues.*

You can use either of the blues scales melodically over blues chords.

Listen to this A blues progression of "I7 IV7," which was used on hits such as "Drive My Car," "Back in the Saddle," "Walk This Way," "In the Midnight Hour," "Rock Me," "Ease on Down the Road," and many others.

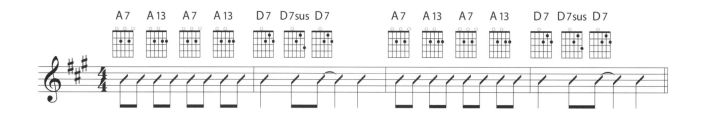

Listen again, and play along with this example. Notice that even though another chord (D7) is added to the A7 groove, it still sounds like it's in the key of A blues.

80 to 85

Writing Exercises

Complete at least one of these exercises. Play and practice it along with one of the drum tracks, or create your own rhythm groove. Use any of the rhythmic tools from unit I to generate your grooves. Transpose the exercises to any blues key.

■ Practice

Create a blues key groove on the progression "I7 IV7."

■ Rewrite the Hits

Choose a 2-chord blues progression from a song you know (or one mentioned in this lesson). Create your own groove to transform it into something new.

■ Create Your Own Melody

Complete the "Practice" or "Rewrite the Hits" exercise above. Create your own melody on top of this groove.

■ Write a Song

Create a song section, with melody and lyrics, using a 2-chord progression in a blues key.

LESSON 14
Colors Outside the Key

Sometimes, you'll feel that a song needs harmonic colors beyond those found in the diatonic chords. We will explore three ways to find chords outside the key that will still sound like natural parts of your harmony.

Hit songs using chords outside the key include "I Was Made to Love Her" [F], "You Are So Beautiful" [C], "Gimme Some Lovin'" [E], "Blackbird" [G], "Help Me Make It through the Night" [C], "You and I" [F], "Johnny Can't Read" [B♭], "Eight Days a Week" [D], "Piano Man" [C], "Sexual Healing" [E♭], "Higher Ground" [E♭ Dorian], "You are the Sunshine of My Life" [C], "Evil Ways" [A Dorian], "Roll on Down the Highway" [C], "Reunited" [C], and many others.

There are three kinds of chord elements that are commonly borrowed from outside the key: the chord's type, root, or secondary dominant. Let's look at each of these.

1. Borrowed *Type*

Borrowing a chord type from outside the key adds nondiatonic notes, which creates different color. To use this tool, simply change the *type* of a diatonic chord.

Listen

Listen to this C major progression. Here, the diatonic F *major7* chord is changed to F7, bringing in the dominant chord color instead. This F7 chord is borrowed from C blues.

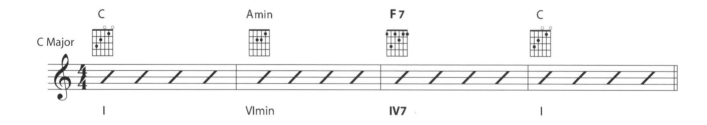

These are the most commonly substituted chord types in the key of C major.

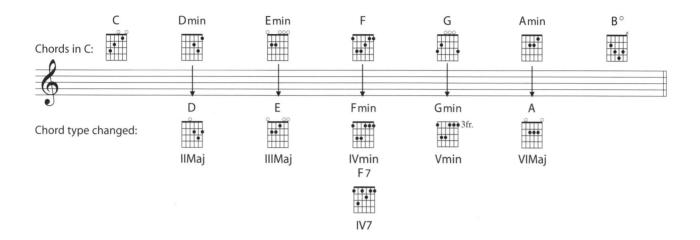

2. Borrowed *Root*

When you borrow a root, you use a chord based on a root that is not in the key.

Listen to this G major progression. The ♭III chord (B♭) is not in the key. It is borrowed from G minor.

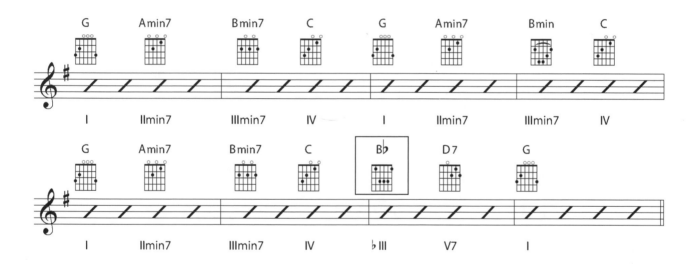

Here are the most commonly borrowed roots in the key of C major.

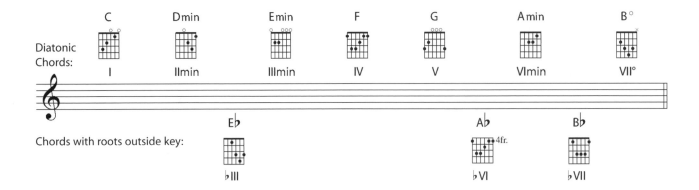

Sources of Borrowed Roots

The most common source of borrowed roots is the progression's *parallel* major or minor key of that same tonic. In a major key, it is most common to borrow roots based on notes from the minor scale: ♭III, ♭VI, and ♭VII.

3. Secondary Dominant Chords

A *secondary dominant* chord (or "secondary V") is a borrowed chord that is a fifth above another diatonic chord in the key.

Listen to this example of a C major groove, and notice how the borrowed D major chord builds tension into the V chord, G. This *secondary dominant* chord (or "secondary V") uses a major chord color outside the key. It is used to build tension towards a chord that isn't the tonic.

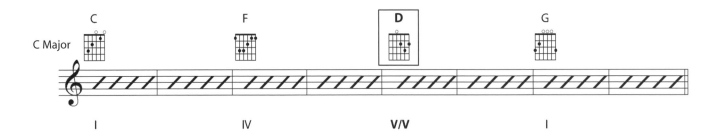

Some of the secondary dominant chords bring out certain emotions in the lyric:

- V/IV brings out a blues emotion.

- V/VImin brings out a gospel or inspirational emotion.

These secondary dominants are commonly used with these chords in the key of C major.

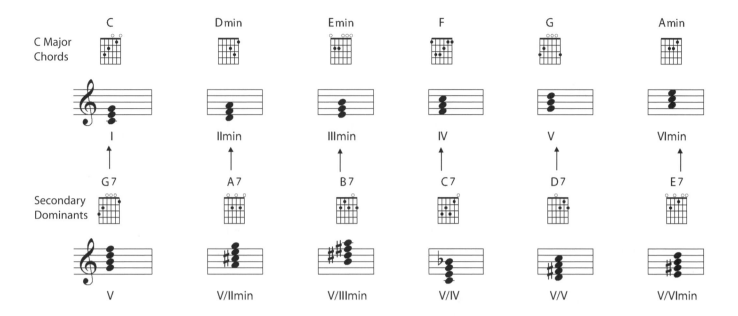

Secondary Dominant Colors

Although secondary dominants are most common in major, you can use a secondary dominant chord of *any* chord, in *any* key. Generally, secondary dominants are either major or seventh chords. Adding the seventh creates even more tension.

Writing Exercises

Complete at least one of these exercises. Play and practice it along with one of the drum tracks, or create your own rhythm groove. Use any of the rhythmic tools from unit I to generate your grooves.

■ Practice

Create a groove on the progression "I V/IV IV IVmin."

■ Rewrite the Hits

Choose a similar progression from a song you know (or one mentioned in this lesson) that uses chords from outside the key. Create your own groove to transform it into something new.

■ Create Your Own Melody

Complete the "Practice" or "Rewrite the Hits" exercise above. Create your own melody on top of this groove.

■ Write a Song

Create a song section, with melody and lyrics, using chords outside the key.

B. Songs from Progressions

In this part, you'll build a song by using a chord progression within a key. Then, you'll learn how to use harmony to contrast sections.

Many of these progressions are so strong that you can create a whole song from them. But adding a contrasting section to it will give you more opportunities for expression and variety.

To create sections that go well together, start by creating a strong groove, using all the tools discussed so far. Then, create a section that contrasts with it, making different choices for each musical element.

LESSON 15
Repetition

In this lesson, you'll learn how use repetition to create a song. It's one of the easiest and most common tools in songwriting.

Hit songs using this tool include "Low Down" [F Dorian], "I Want a New Drug" [A Mixolydian], "Don't Stop" [F Mixolydian], "Oye Como Va" [A Dorian], "I Wish" [E♭ Dorian], "Norwegian Wood" [E Mixolydian], "Imagine" [C], "You Sexy Thing" [F], "Don't Stop" [E♭ Mixolydian], "Feelin' Alright" [C Blues], "Shakin' the Tree" [E♭], "No Woman No Cry" [C], and many others.

Notice how repetition of the following progressions creates a whole section or a whole song.

"Feeling Alright"

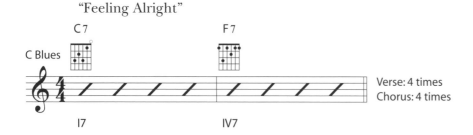

"Walking on the Moon"

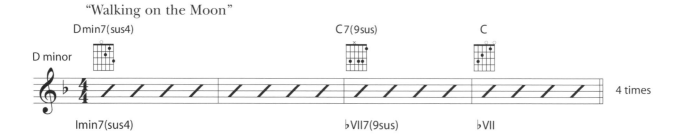

"Low Down"

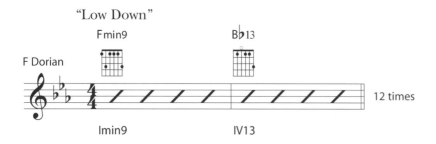

Listen

Listen to this example created from the "I7 IV7" blues progression, the same one used in "Feelin' Alright," "Drive My Car," and "In the Midnight Hour." Here, it is transposed to A blues. Notice how the blues key color captures the bluesy, sexy emotion of the lyric.

Listen again and play and/or sing along. Notice the way both the verse and the chorus are built by simply repeating the progression four times. Also notice the way the melody contrasts in the verse and the chorus. For more on melodic tools for contrast, see *The Songwriter's Workshop: Melody.*

Writing Exercises

Complete at least one of these exercises. Play and practice it along with one of the drum tracks, or create your own rhythm groove. Use any of the rhythmic tools from unit I to generate your grooves.

■ Practice

Choose any progression from this book, and create a song section (or a whole song) by repeating it two, four, or eight times.

■ Rewrite the Hits

Choose a chord progression from a song you know (or one mentioned in this lesson). Create a song section or whole song using simple repetition.

■ Create Your Own Melody

Complete the "Practice" or "Rewrite the Hits" exercise above. Create your own melody on top of this groove.

■ Write a Song

Create a song, with melody and lyrics, by using simple repetition of a chord progression.

LESSON 16
Contrasting Sections

You can also use different chord colors to create song sections that contrast.

Hit songs using this tool include "Sweet Emotion" [A], "Bang a Drum" [E], and "Walk This Way" [C blues].

In the following example, notice how the 2-chord chorus contrasts with the 1-chord verse by using a chord progression. The different chord rhythms help make each section sound distinct.

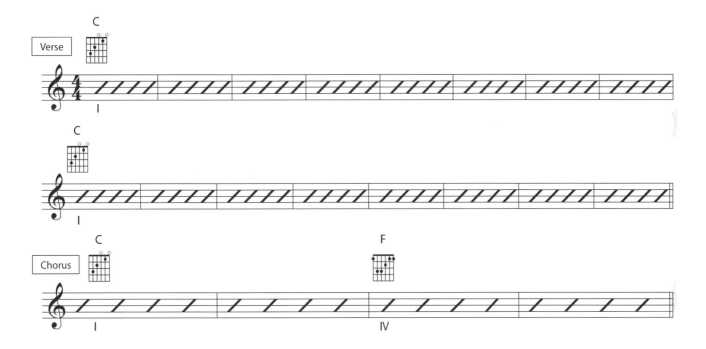

Listen

25 Listen to this Mixolydian song. Notice how the 1-chord groove in the verse contrasts with the chorus's chord progression, "I ♭VII." Then, listen again, and play and/or sing along.

She's got a way to move___ me   She's so sweet and fine_____

When I'm with her   I   think I'm spe - cial   Just like a real fine wine____

Oo_____ Sweet A - man - da___

Oo_____ Sweet A - man - da___

Writing Exercises

Complete at least one of these exercises. Play and practice it along with one of the drum tracks, or create your own rhythm groove. Use any of the rhythmic tools from unit I to generate your grooves.

■ Practice

Create two contrasting sections using a 1-chord groove in the verse and a chord progression in the chorus.

■ Rewrite the Hits

Choose a 1-chord groove from a song you know (or one mentioned in this lesson). Create a contrasting section using a different, original progression, or one from a different song.

■ Create Your Own Melody

Complete the "Practice" or "Rewrite the Hits" exercise above. Create your own melody on top of this groove.

■ Write a Song

Create two contrasting sections with melody and lyrics. Use a 1-chord groove in the verse, and contrast it with a chord progression in the chorus.

UNIT IV
Power Progressions

Certain chord progressions have been used in countless songs. There seems to be something powerful about these chord progressions—something that makes them memorable. Memorizing these "power progressions," varying them, and using them gives you an easy source of ideas that have been tested and proven.

In this unit, you'll learn some of these power progressions. Each key color has its own power progressions associated with it. The progressions you learned in unit III are actually 2-chord power progressions.

After you learn these power progressions, you'll use them to build songs.

Chord Charts

The appendix provides chord charts for every key, in every transposition. Use these charts to transpose the power progressions to all keys.

A. Power Progressions in the Five Key Colors

In part A, you'll learn power progressions in each of the five key colors. Learning these progressions will give you a huge amount of material from which to build your songs.

These progressions are described by Roman numerals, which stand for the scale degree on which the chords are based. The progressions can be applied to any key. To find actual chords, see the charts in the appendix, but familiarize yourself with this Roman numeral shorthand so that you can find the chords without having to refer to the charts.

The progressions are presented in their simplest, most essential forms. As you get to know them, you should incorporate all the variations in grooves, notes, chords, and so on that we have been discussing throughout this book.

LESSON 17
Major-Key Power Progressions

Following are the most common major-key power progressions and some hits songs that use them. (Note: All progressions are presented in the key of C major.)

I	IV
C	F

"Endless Love" [B♭], "I Want to Hold Your Hand" [G], "Help Me Make It through the Night" [C], "Gone Country" [C]

I	IV	V
C	F	G

"Like a Rolling Stone" [C], "Twist and Shout" [F], "River of Dreams" [G], "I Love Rock and Roll" [E], "Here Comes the Sun" [A], "Rock and Roll All Nite" [A], "Tonight I Celebrate My Love" [E♭], "Tracks of My Tears" [G]

I	VImin	IImin	V
C	Amin	Dmin	G

Common Variations

I	VImin	IV	V
C	Amin	F	G

IIImin	VImin	IImin	V
Emin	Amin	Dmin	G

"Savin' All My Love for You" [A], "Earth Angel" [E♭], "This Boy" [D], "I'll Make Love to You" [D], "Please Mister Postman" [A], "If You Really Love Me" [C], "Superwoman" [E♭], "Breezin'" [D], "In the Still of the Night" [C]

I	IImin	IIImin	IV
C	Dmin	Emin	F

"Here There and Everywhere" [G], "Longer" [G], "Lean on Me" [C]

I	V/7*	VImin	I/5	IV	I/3	IImin	V
C	G/B	Amin	C/G	F	C/E	Dmin	G

"Piano Man" [C], "Mister Bojangles" [D], "Let It Be" [F], "I'll Be There" [F]

*Arabic numerals indicate the note *in the key*.

Listen

 Listen to this example, using each major-key power progression in turn.

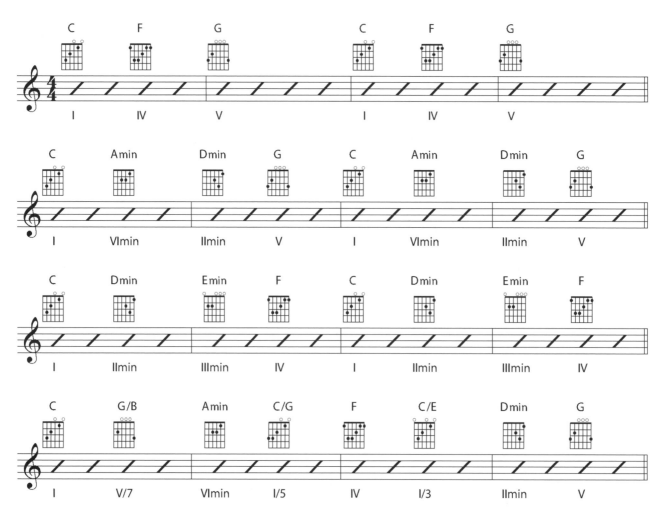

Listen again, and play along with the track. Like the other progressions you have learned, each of these power progressions can be used to build a song section or a complete song. So, memorize these progressions, and play them in different keys. They will lead you to many strong song ideas.

 Now, listen to this example based on the "I IImin IIImin IV" power progression in G. Notice how the chords in this progression seem to climb up the scale.

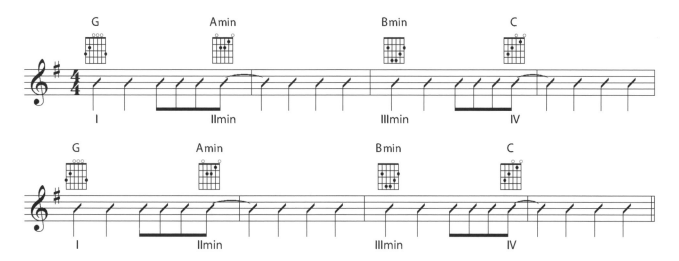

Listen again, and play along. Notice that this progression is played twice to make a song section.

Writing Exercises

 Complete at least one of these exercises. Play and practice it along with one of the drum tracks, or create your own rhythm groove. Use any of the rhythmic tools from unit I to generate your grooves.

■ Practice

Create a major-key groove using one of the power progressions in this lesson.

■ Rewrite the Hits

Choose a hit song that is based on one of these major-key power progressions. Create your own groove using a similar power progression.

■ Create Your Own Melody

Complete either the "Practice" or "Rewrite the Hits" exercise above. Then create your own melody to go with this progression.

■ Write a Song

Create a song section, with melody and lyrics, using one of the progressions in this lesson.

LESSON 18
Minor-Key Power Progressions

These are the most common minor-key power progressions, with some of the songs that are based upon them. (Note: All progressions are presented in the key of A minor.)

Imin **♭VII**
Amin   G

"King of Pain" [Bmin], "We Are the Champions" [Cmin], "Walking on the Moon" [Dmin], "Ohio" [Amin], "Where Have All the Cowboys Gone?" [F♯min], "Wrapped around Your Finger" [Amin]

Imin **♭VII** **♭VI** **♭VII**
Amin   G   F   G

Common Variation

Imin **♭VII** **♭VI** **V**
Amin   G   F   E

"All Along the Watchtower" [Amin], "Standin' in the Shadows of Love" [Amin], "Remember [Walking in the Sand]" [Cmin], "Happy Together" [Amin], "Love Child" [B♭min]

Imin **Vmin**
Amin   Emin

"Things We Said Today" [Gmin], "Where Have All the Cowboys Gone?" [F♯min]

Imin **IVmin**
Amin   Dmin

"I Shot the Sheriff" [Gmin], "Another One Bites the Dust" [Amin], "Boogie Wonderland" [Dmin]

Listen

28 Listen to this example, using each minor-key power progression in turn. Then listen again, and play along with the track. Each progression can be used to build a song section or a complete song. Memorize them all, and practice them in different keys.

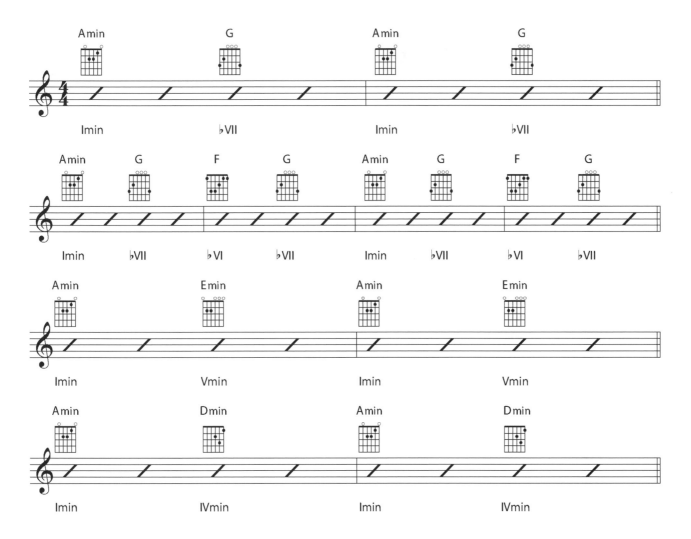

29 Now, listen to this power progression in E minor, and notice how the chords go down and up the scale. This strong line makes the progression so easily identifiable and powerful.

Listen again, and play along with the track. Notice that the progression is played four times to make a song section.

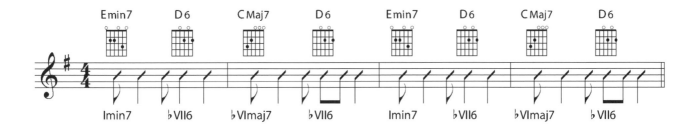

Writing Exercises

Complete at least one of these exercises. Play and practice it along with one of the drum tracks, or create your own rhythm groove. Use any of the rhythmic tools from unit I to generate your grooves.

■ Practice

Create a minor-key groove using one of the power progressions in this lesson.

■ Rewrite the Hits

Choose a hit song that is based on one of these minor-key power progressions. Create your own groove using a similar power progression.

■ Create Your Own Melody

Complete either the "Practice" or "Rewrite the Hits" exercise above. Then create your own melody to go with this progression.

■ Write a Song

Create a song section, with melody and lyrics, using one of the progressions in this lesson.

LESSON 19
Mixolydian-Key Power Progressions

These are the most common Mixolydian-key power progressions, with some hit songs that use them. (Note: All progressions are presented in the key of C Mixoloydian.)

I	♭VII
C	B♭

"Paperback Writer" [G Mixolydian], "Manic Depression" [A Mixolydian], "Fire" [D Mixolydian] "Reelin' in the Years" [A Mixolydian], "Only You Know and I Know" [E♭ Mixolydian], "Tears of a Clown" [D♭ Mixolydian], "Don't Stop 'til You Get Enough" [C Mixolydian], "Norwegian Wood" [E Mixolydian], "Saturday Night's Alright" [G Mixolydian and C Mixolydian], "My Generation" [F Mixolydian], "Centerfold" [G Mixolydian], "Boogie Fever" [F Mixolydian], "Hollywood Nights" [E Mixolydian]

I	♭VII	IV
C	B♭	F

"Shake Your Body Down to the Ground" [E♭ Mixolydian], "I Want a New Drug" [A Mixolydian], "Ghostbusters" [B Mixolydian], "Boogie On Reggae Woman" [A♭ Mixolydian], "Gloria" [E Mixolydian], "Last Time" [E Mixolydian]

Listen

Listen to this power progression in E Mixolydian. Then listen again, and play along with the track. Notice that the whole section is based on repeating the same progression four times. In many Mixolydian songs, the whole tune uses only this progression. Memorize it, and practice it in different keys.

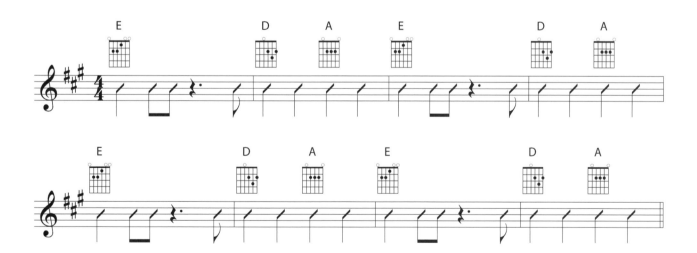

Writing Exercises

Complete at least one of these exercises. Play and practice it along with one of the drum tracks, or create your own rhythm groove. Use any of the rhythmic tools from unit I to generate your grooves.

■ Practice

Create a Mixolydian-key groove using one of the power progressions in this lesson.

■ Rewrite the Hits

Choose a hit song that is based on one of these Mixolydian-key power progressions. Create your own groove using a similar power progression.

■ Create Your Own Melody

Complete either the "Practice" or "Rewrite the Hits" exercise above. Then create your own melody to go with this progression.

■ Write a Song

Create a song section, with melody and lyrics, using one of the progressions in this lesson.

LESSON 20
Dorian-Key Power Progressions

These are the most common Dorian-key power progressions, and some hit songs that use them. (Note: All progressions are presented in the key of D Dorian.)

Imin   IV
Dmin   G

"Evil Ways" [A Dorian], "I Wish" [E♭ Dorian], "Lowdown" [F Dorian], "Foxy Lady" [F♯ Dorian], "Owner of a Lonely Heart" [A Dorian], "Moondance" [A Dorian], "Billie Jean" [F♯ Dorian]

Imin   IImin   ♭III   IImin
Dmin   Emin   F   Emin

"Billie Jean" [F♯ Dorian], "Moondance" [A Dorian]

Listen

Listen to this example based on a power progression in A Dorian. Then listen again, and play along with the track. Notice that the whole section is based on repeating the same progression four times. In many Dorian songs, a section, or sometimes a whole song, often uses only this progression. Memorize it, and practice it in different keys.

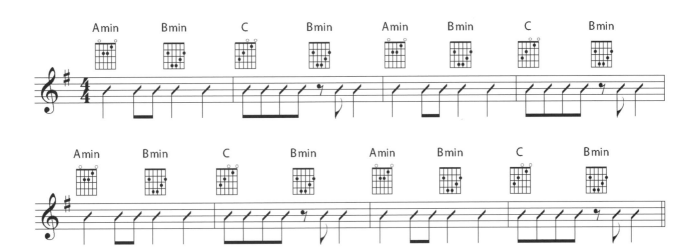

Writing Exercises

80 to 85

Complete at least one of these exercises. Play and practice it along with one of the drum tracks, or create your own rhythm groove. Use any of the rhythmic tools from unit I to generate your grooves.

■ Practice

Create a Dorian-key groove using one of the power progressions in this lesson.

■ Rewrite the Hits

Choose a hit song that is based on one of these Dorian-key power progressions. Create your own groove using a similar power progression.

■ Create Your Own Melody

Complete either the "Practice" or "Rewrite the Hits" exercise above. Then create your own melody to go with this progression.

■ Write a Song

Create a song section, with melody and lyrics, using one of the progressions in this lesson.

LESSON 21
Blues-Key Power Progressions

The blues key color has three power progressions, including the "I7 IV7" progression discussed in lesson 13. Of the other two, one is a simple repetitive progression, and one is a long, 12-measure progression. (Note: All progressions are presented in the key of C blues.)

Repetitive Progressions

I7	IV7	
C7	F7	

I7	♭III	IV
C7	E♭	F

"Higher Ground" [E♭], "Purple Haze" [E], "I Can See for Miles" [E], "Born to Be Wild" [G]

Listen

Listen to this "I♭III IV" power progression. Then listen again, and play along. Notice that the whole section is based on repeating the same progression four times. Practice it in many different keys.

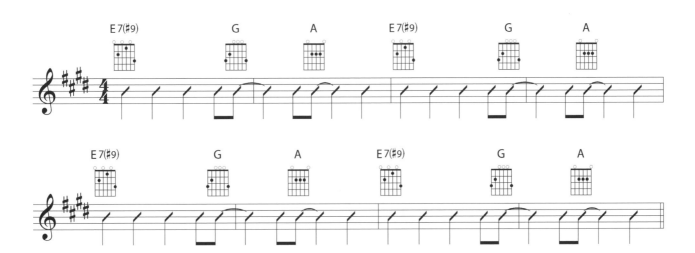

12-Bar Blues

The most common blues progression is called the "12-bar blues." It is twelve measures long, with the chords in this order.

I7	**IV7**	**I7**	**V7**	**IV7**	**I7**	**(V7)**
C7	F7	C7	G7	F7	C7	(G7)

"Johnny B. Goode" [A], "Can't Buy Me Love" [C], "Pink Cadillac" [E], "She's a Woman" [A], "Dancin' in the Dark" [C], "Still Haven't Found What I'm Looking For" [D], "I Feel Good" [D], "Sunshine of Your Love" [D], "Birthday" [A], "Boys" [E], "Day Tripper" [E], "You Can't Do That" [C], "Change the World" [F], "Gimme One Reason" [G], "Life in the Fast Lane" [E], "Hey, Hey, Hey" [G], and many, many others.

 Listen to this 12-bar blues in A. Then listen again, and play along.

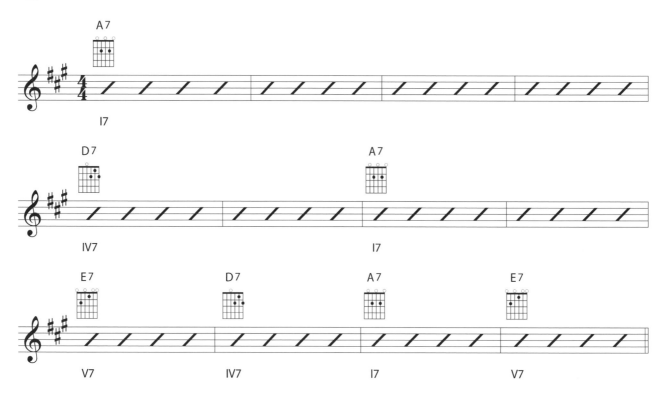

Notice some unique things about this progression:

■ It's twelve measures long, in three phrases.

■ Each phrase starts on a different chord.

■ Each phrase has a different harmonic rhythm.

■ The last phrase has a blues *cadence:* it comes "home" to the tonic chord.

The 12-bar blues is one of your most important resources. Learn it in all keys, and try adding notes to the chords (see unit II). The blues form can be adapted to any style.

Writing Exercises

Complete at least one of these exercises. Play and practice it along with one of the drum tracks, or create your own rhythm groove. Use any of the rhythmic tools from unit I to generate your grooves.

■ Practice

Create a blues groove using one of the power progressions in this lesson. If you use one of the shorter progressions, repeat it to create a song section. If you use the 12-bar blues, once through is enough.

■ Rewrite the Hits

Choose a hit song that is based on one of these blues power progressions. Create your own groove using a similar power progression.

■ Create Your Own Melody

Complete either the "Practice" or "Rewrite the Hits" exercise above. Then create your own melody to go with this progression.

■ Write a Song

Create a song section, with melody and lyrics, using one of the progressions in this lesson.

B. Building Song Sections

In unit III, you learned how to build song sections by repeating a chord progression. Now, we'll learn some to build song sections using two power progressions. Then, we'll develop two contrasting sections, using two different power progressions.

Though we are using the power progressions to demonstrate these procedures, you can use them on any chord progressions.

Practice Using Power Progressions

Practice building song sections out of power progressions. You'll get a lot of mileage out of them.

LESSON 22
One Section, Two Progressions

In addition to simple repetition, you can build a song section by combining two power progressions. There are a variety of ways to do this.

Hit songs that combine two power progressions within a section include "Night Shift" [G], "Wind Beneath My Wings" [G], "Lady Madonna" [A], and many others.

You can use the two progressions in many ways. Here are two ways: in pairs, and alternating. (In these diagrams, P1 stands for the first power progression, and P2 for the second.)

1. Pairs: P1 + P1 + P2 + P2

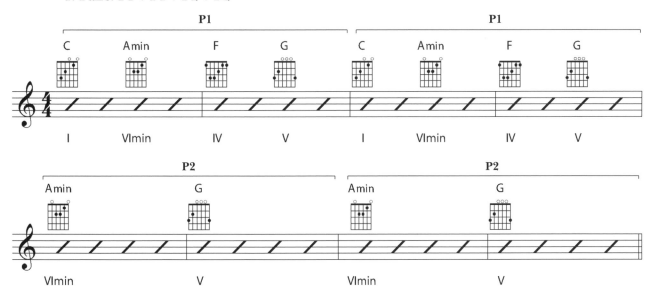

2. Alternating: P1 + P2 + P1 + P2

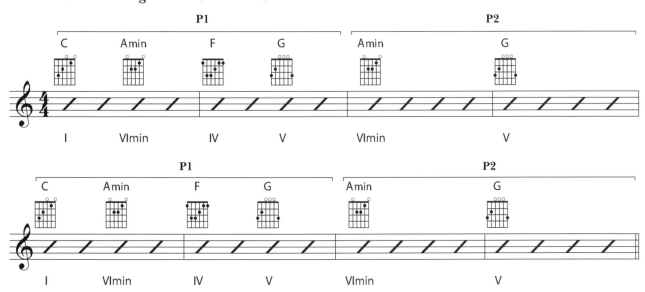

Listen

Listen to this example, which illustrates alternating progressions P1 and P2. Notice that together, the two power progressions make a longer, 4-measure progression. Then, this 4-measure progression is repeated to make an 8-measure chorus.

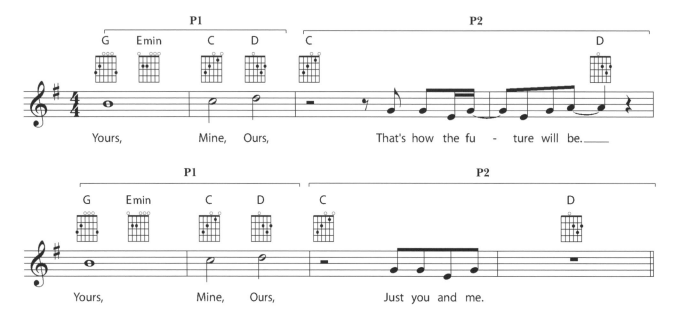

Listen again, and play along with the recording. Notice how the song goes to the V chord (D) a little later in bars 4 and 8, and how the major-key color brings out the positive lyric emotion.

This section is a chorus. The title is usually set differently than the rest of the lines. How is the melody of the title "Yours, Mine, Ours" different than the other phrases?

Writing Exercises

Complete at least one of these exercises. Play and practice it along with one of the drum tracks, or create your own rhythm groove. Use any of the rhythmic tools from unit I to generate your grooves.

■ Practice

Create either a verse or a chorus by combining two different power progressions from part A of this unit. Combine them in either of the ways above, or any way you like.

■ Rewrite the Hits

Choose two progressions from songs you know (or ones mentioned in this lesson). Create a song section by combining them in either of the ways above or any way you like.

■ Create Your Own Melody

Complete either the "Practice" or "Rewrite the Hits" exercise above. Then create your own melody to go over these progressions.

■ Write a Song

Create a song section, with melody and lyrics, that combines two power progressions.

LESSON 23
Two Sections, Two Progressions

Using contrasting progressions is a great way to contrast two sections, such as a verse and chorus.

Hit songs with contrasting progressions between sections include "Wind Beneath My Wings" [G], "Like a Rolling Stone" [C], "Can't Buy Me Love" [C], and many others.

Listen

Listen to this example, which uses two different blues power progressions. The verse is a variation of the 12-bar blues, while the chorus uses the progression "I ♭III IV."

Listen again, and then play along with the track. Notice that the sections contrast by using:

- different progressions

- different chords

- different progression lengths

How is the melody different in the verse and chorus? Notice the way the blues key color reflects the lyric.

Writing Exercises

Complete at least one of these exercises. Play and practice it along with one of the drum tracks, or create your own rhythm groove. Use any of the rhythmic tools from unit I to generate your grooves.

■ Practice

Create two contrasting sections using two different power progressions. Use any progressions you have learned so far.

■ Rewrite the Hits

Choose two different power progressions from any songs you know (or ones mentioned in this unit)—preferably, progressions of different lengths. Create two contrasting sections out of these progressions.

■ Create Your Own Melody

Complete either the "Practice" or "Rewrite the Hits" exercise above. Then create your own melody to go over these progressions.

■ Write a Song

Create two contrasting sections, with melody and lyrics, over two different chord progressions of different lengths.

UNIT V
Rhythm Variations of Progressions

In the next two units, you'll learn how to vary chord progressions, which can lead you to an infinite number of harmonic ideas for your songs. We will explore two types of variation: rhythm and pitch.

Once you learn these tools, you will be able to generate many different variations of the same progression, whether it be a power progression or any other chord progression you wish to use as the basis for something new.

A. Rhythm Variations of Progressions

We begin by studying how rhythm can be used to vary chord progressions. Each lesson shows how some great songs were created using rhythm variations of common power progressions.

We will explore three types of rhythm variations:

■ changing the *length* of the progression

■ changing the *rhythm* of one or more of the chords

■ changing the *order* of the chords

Using these rhythm tools and the various tools from earlier units, you will be able to create countless songs out of a single chord progression.

LESSON 24
Progression Length

You can change the length of a chord progression to create anything from a 2-beat progression to a complete 8-measure section.

Hit songs that are all rhythm variations of a "I VImin IImin V" progression include "Superwoman" [A♭], "Breezin'" [D], "In the Still of the Night" [C], "Miracle" [G], "I'll Make Love to You" [D], "Up on the Roof" [G], "We're in This Love Together" [B♭], "Please Mister Postman" [A], "Mercy, Mercy Me" [E], and many others.

Listen

Listen to these different versions of the "I IV" progression. As used in the tune "Imagine" and so many others, there are four beats on each chord, in a 2-measure harmonic phrase.

Original

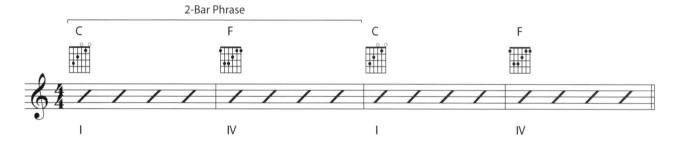

There are several ways to change the length of a progression. Consider the major-key progression "I IV." Notice how all these songs vary the length of the original.

Variation 1

You can play it at a *faster rhythm*, or "shrink it" to two beats on each chord, a 1-measure harmonic phrase, and you get "In the Midnight Hour."

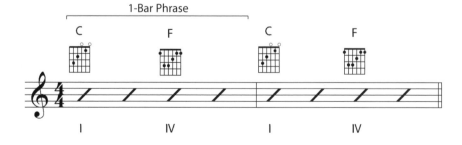

Variation 2

Play it at an even faster rhythm—one beat on each chord, half-measure phrase—and you get "Hey, Hey, Hey" and "The Way You Do the Things You Do."

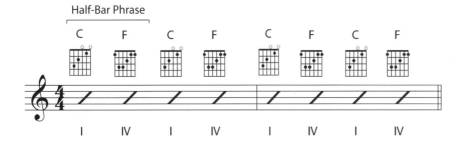

Variation 3

Play it at a *slower rhythm*, or "stretch it out"—two measures on each chord, 4-measure phrase—and you'll get "Shining Star."

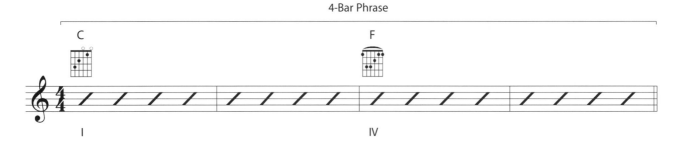

Listen

Listen to this example based on the Dorian progression "Imin7 IV7." The progression is stretched out to four measures.

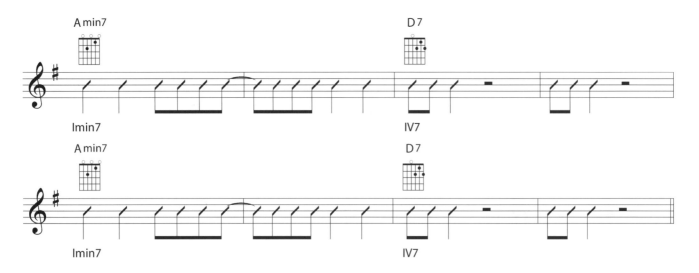

Listen again, and play along with the recording. Notice that the rhythmic phrase, combining two motives, is also four measures long.

Writing Exercises

Complete at least one of these exercises. Play and practice it along with one of the drum tracks, or create your own rhythm groove. Use any of the rhythmic tools from unit I to generate your grooves.

■ Practice

Create a groove by changing the length of the "Imin7 IV7" progression or any progression of your choice.

■ Rewrite the Hits

Choose a progression from a song you know (or a song mentioned in this lesson). Change the length of the original progression to transform it into your original song.

■ Create Your Own Melody

Transform any progression you know by changing its length, and then create your own melody over it.

■ Write a Song

Complete the "Create Your Own Melody" exercise above, and add lyrics.

LESSON 25
Chord Rhythm

Changing the rhythm of just part of the progression—one or more of the chords—is another source of possible variations.

Hit songs that vary the rhythm of only part of a common progression include "King of Pain" [D], "Ain't Too Proud to Beg" [C], "River of Dreams" [G], "I Love Rock and Roll" [E], "Here Comes the Sun" [A], "Rock and Roll All Nite" [A], "Tonight I Celebrate My Love" [E♭], "Tracks of My Tears" [G], "Endless Love" [B♭], and many others.

Listen

In the previous lesson, we changed the rhythm by changing the entire progression, uniformly. Now, we are only changing the rhythm of part of the progression. To use this tool, play one or more of the chords for a different number of beats.

Listen to this common setting of the power progression "I IV V."

Original

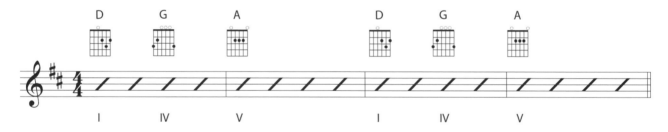

Listen to each of these variations, and notice how the rhythm of only part of the progression was changed to create something used in different songs.

Variation 1
"River of Dreams," "I Love Rock and Roll," "Here Comes the Sun," "Rock and Roll All Nite"

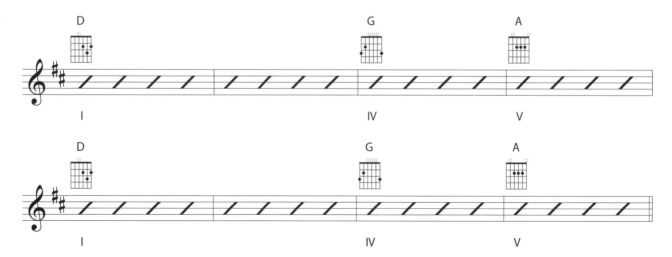

Variation 2
"Tonight I Celebrate My Love," "I Love Rock and Roll"

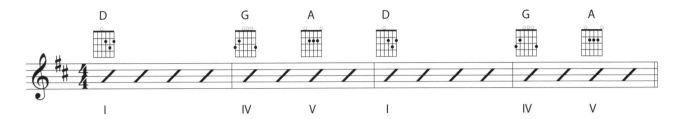

Variation 3
"Tracks of My Tears"

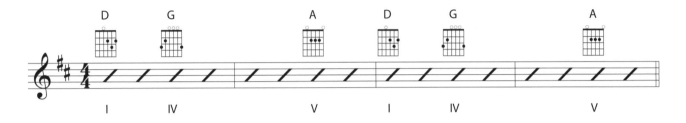

 Listen to this common 1-measure setting of the Mixolydian power progression
"I ♭VII IV."

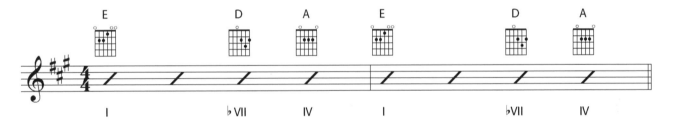

Then, listen to this example, which stretches out the I chord.

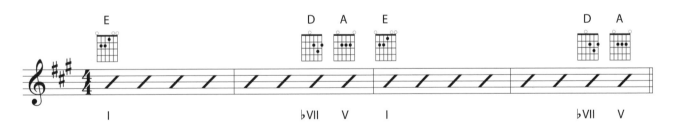

Listen again, and play along with the recording. Notice that the progression is now
two measures long.

Writing Exercises

Complete at least one of these exercises. Play and practice it along with one of the drum tracks, or create your own rhythm groove. Use any of the rhythmic tools from unit I to generate your grooves.

■ Practice

Create a groove by changing the rhythm of any of the chords in the "I IV V" or "I ♭VII V" progression or any progression of your choice.

■ Rewrite the Hits

Choose a progression from a song you know (or a song mentioned in this lesson). Change the rhythm of any of its chords to create your own groove.

■ Create Your Own Melody

Transform any progression you know by changing the rhythm of any of its chords, and then create your own melody over it.

■ Write a Song

Complete the "Create Your Own Melody" exercise above, and add lyrics.

LESSON 26
Chord Order

Changing the *order* of chords can transform a common progression into something new.

Hit songs based on changing the chord order of a common progression include "Exhale" [C], "You're in My Heart" [B], "Already Gone" [C], "Helpless" [D], "Sweet Home Alabama" [D], "The Wind Cries Mary" [F], and many others.

Listen

Listen to these different versions of the common "I IV V" progression. Here's how it was used in such tunes as "Like a Rolling Stone."

Original

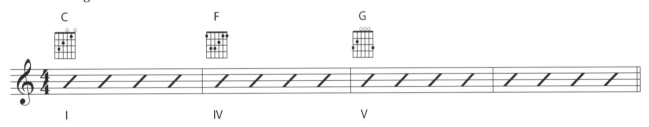

Variation 1

Play it backwards and you get the progression used in tunes such as "Sweet Home Alabama" and "The Wind Cries Mary."

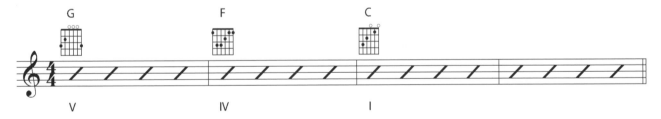

Variation 2

Mix it up differently, and get the variation used in "Already Gone" and "Helpless."

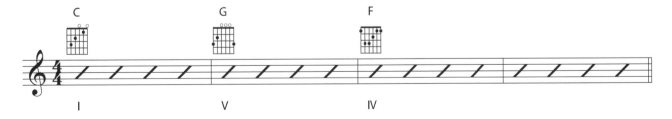

Listen to this example based on the Mixolydian progression "I ♭VII IV." Notice how the order of the chords "I IV ♭VII" is changed, along with the length and chord rhythm of the original progression.

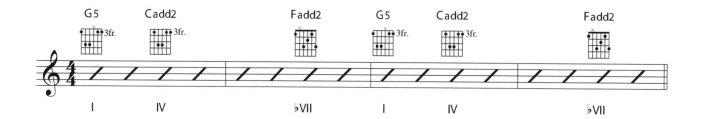

Listen again, and play along with the recording.

Writing Exercises

 Complete at least one of these exercises. Play and practice it along with one of the drum tracks, or create your own rhythm groove. Use any of the rhythmic tools from unit I to generate your grooves.

■ Practice

Create a groove by changing the chord order of a "I IV V" or "I IV ♭VII" progression or any progression of your choice.

■ Rewrite the Hits

Choose a progression from a song you know (or a song mentioned in this lesson). Change the order of chords to transform it into your original song.

■ Create Your Own Melody

Transform any progression you know by changing the order, and then create your own melody over it.

■ Write a Song

Complete the "Create Your Own Melody" exercise above, and add lyrics.

B. Building Song Sections

In part B of this unit, you'll learn some ways to create two and three contrasting sections using rhythm variations of chord progressions.

LESSON 27
Rhythmic Contrast: Two Sections from One Progression

Creating two contrasting sections from two different rhythm variations of the same chord progression is a great way get a lot of mileage out of the same progression. Using the same progression helps the song sections to sound related, while varying the rhythm adds enough contrast to keep the song sounding interesting.

Hit songs that create contrast by varying a progression's rhythm include "Satisfaction" [E], "Shout" [C], "Ain't Too Proud to Beg" [G], "You Can't Hurry Love" [B♭], "China Grove" [E], and many others.

In the following songs, notice that the different sections are just rhythm variations of the same progression.

In the style of "Satisfaction"

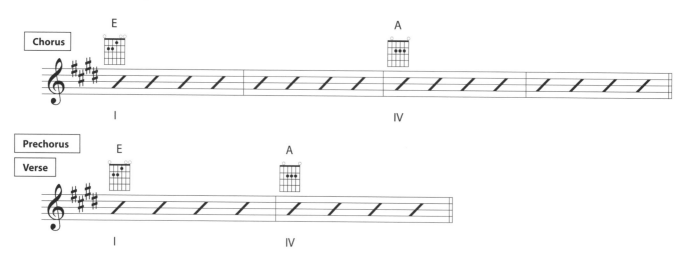

In the style of "Shout"

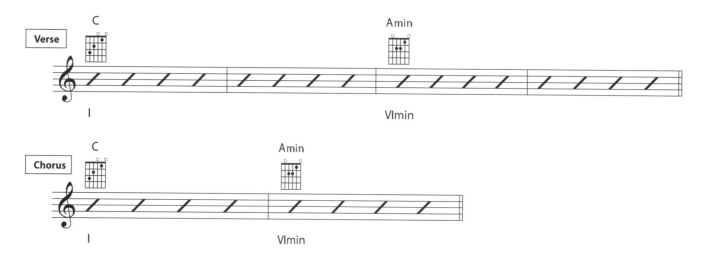

In the style of "Ain't Too Proud to Beg"

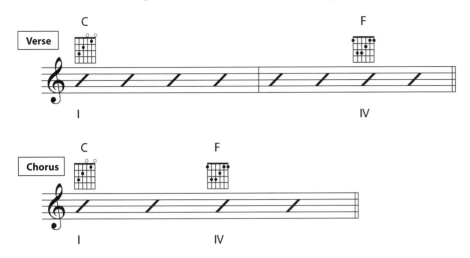

In the style of "China Grove"

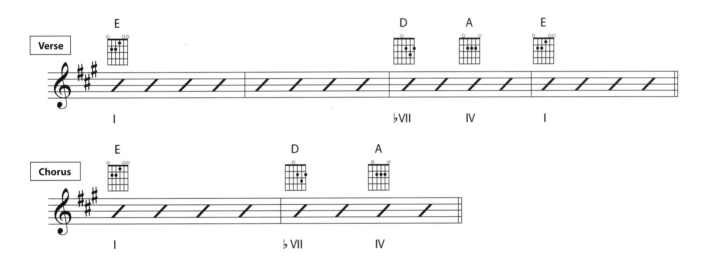

Listen

Listen to this example. It uses two different rhythm variations of the "Imin IV7" Dorian progression. Notice that using the same chords makes the sections sound unified, but the contrasting variations make them sound distinct, keeping each new section sounding fresh.

Listen again, and play along with the recording. How is the melody different in the verse and chorus?

Writing Exercises

Complete at least one of these exercises. Play and practice it along with one of the drum tracks, or create your own rhythm groove. Use any of the rhythmic tools from unit I to generate your grooves.

■ Practice

Create two contrasting sections using two different rhythm variations of the "I IV" progression or any progression of your choice.

■ Rewrite the Hits

Choose a progression from a song you know (or a song mentioned in this lesson). Create two contrasting sections by using two rhythm variations of this progression.

■ Create Your Own Melody

Complete either the "Practice" or "Rewrite the Hits" exercise above. Then create your own melody over these two sections.

■ Write a Song

Complete the "Create Your Own Melody" exercise above, and add lyrics.

LESSON 28
Two Sections, Two Progressions

You can create further contrast between sections by using contrasting chord progressions in each one. Choosing progressions that begin on different chords creates even more contrast, as does choosing progressions that have different chord rhythms—both the length of the harmonic phrase, and the individual chord rhythms. You can also choose progressions that are not common power progressions.

Hit songs that use contrasting progressions in each section include "Rock Me" [C], "Bang a Drum" [E], and many others.

Listen

Listen to this tune that uses two contrasting progressions. Notice that the verse uses the "I7 IV7" blues progression, and the chorus uses the "I♭III IV" blues progression, though reordered as "♭III IV I." There are several ways that these two progressions contrast:

- They start on different chords.

- They are different lengths.

- They contrast chord rhythms.

All of these ways of contrasting help the audience to hear the difference in sections.

Listen again, and play along with the recording. The sections also contrast by using power chords in the chorus, as opposed to seventh chords in the verse. How is the melody different in the verse and chorus?

Writing Exercises

Complete at least one of these exercises. Play and practice it along with one of the drum tracks, or create your own rhythm groove. Use any of the rhythmic tools from unit I to generate your grooves.

The rhythm variations you develop should start on different chords, be of different lengths, and use different chord rhythms.

■ Practice

Create two contrasting sections using rhythm variations of two different chord progressions.

■ Rewrite the Hits

Choose two progressions from songs you know (or a song mentioned in this lesson). Create two contrasting sections based on these progressions.

■ Create Your Own Melody

Complete the "Practice" or "Rewrite the Hits" exercises above, and add your own melody to them.

■ Write a Song

Complete the "Create Your Own Melody" exercise above, and add your own lyrics.

LESSON 29
A Contrasting Prechorus

Many songs use the same progression in the verse and chorus. Often, the *prechorus* (song section leading to the chorus) is written last and inserted between the harmonically similar verse and chorus. You can use the rhythmic tools you learned so far to contrast, and build excitement, in the prechorus.

Hit songs with a contrasting prechorus include "How Will I Know" [G♭], "Billie Jean" [F♯ Dorian], and many others.

Listen

Listen to this example. Both the verse and chorus use "I IV V." The prechorus changes the order of "IImin IIImin IV V" to "IV IIImin IImin V." Starting the prechorus on a different chord adds further contrast with the verse and chorus.

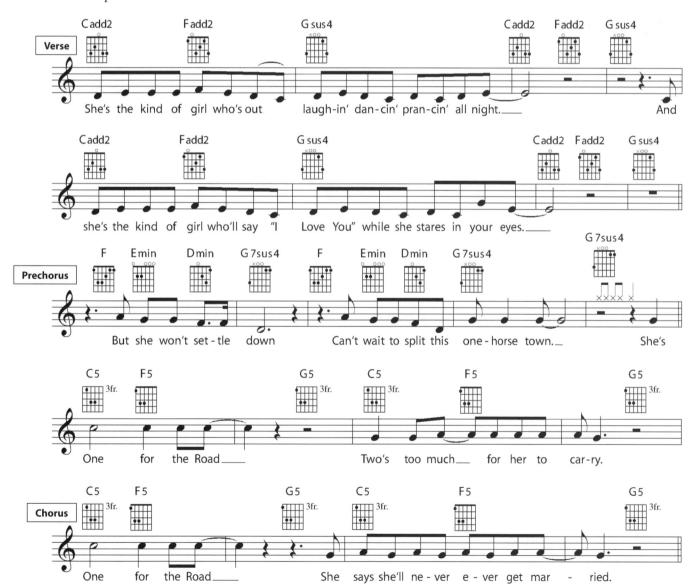

Listen again, and play along with the recording. Notice that the chorus varies the verse groove by using power chords and by subtly changing the rhythmic feel. In addition, the progressions start on different chords, and the chord rhythms are different. How is the melody different in the verse and chorus?

Writing Exercises

Complete at least one of these exercises. Play and practice it along with one of the drum tracks, or create your own rhythm groove. Use any of the rhythmic tools from unit I to generate your grooves.

Build excitement in the prechorus by using a shorter phrase length and/or changing chords faster.

■ Practice

Create a verse/prechorus/chorus song with two chord progressions: one in the verse and chorus, and the other in the prechorus. Use the "I IV V" and "IImin IIImin IV V" progressions or any progressions of your choice.

■ Rewrite the Hits

Create a verse and chorus using a chord progression from a hit song. Then create a contrasting prechorus to lead from the verse to the chorus.

■ Create Your Own Melody

Complete the "Practice" or "Rewrite the Hits" exercise above. Create your own melody.

■ Write a Song

Complete the "Practice" or "Rewrite the Hits" exercises above. Create your own melody, with lyrics, for each of the three different sections.

UNIT VI
Pitch Variations of Progressions

Another way to create new ideas out of the power progressions, or any chord progression, is to change the actual chords in them. Like the rhythm variations, modifying the pitches gives the benefits of using the tried-and-true progression, while adding enough new material to keep it sounding fresh. This unit explores some of the ways to use pitch as a source of variations.

A. Pitch Variations of Progressions

In part A, we will explore four ways of varying a progression by using pitch:

- subtracting a chord from the original progression

- adding a chord to the original progression

- replacing a chord in the original progression

- adding a repetitive melodic idea, called a *pedal*, to the original progression

LESSON 30
Subtract Chords

You can subtract (omit) chords from a progression to create a new one with a different character.

Hit songs created by subtracting a chord from a progression include "Angel" [A Dorian], "Girls Just Want to Have Fun" [G♭], "Some Like It Hot" [Emin], and many others.

Here is a common Dorian progression, "Imin IImin ♭III IImin," which was used in tunes such as "Moondance," "Billie Jean," and many others.

Original

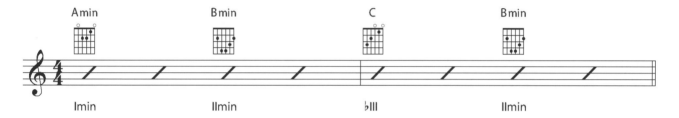

By subtracting the last chord, we get a new progression, used in tunes such as "Angel."

Variation

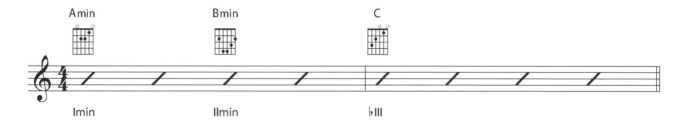

Here is a common power progression, "Imin ♭VII ♭VI ♭VII," used in tunes such as "All Along the Watchtower."

Original

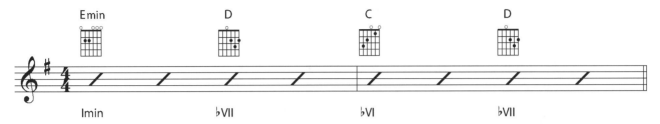

By subtracting the second chord (D), we get the progression used in tunes such as "Some Like It Hot."

Variation

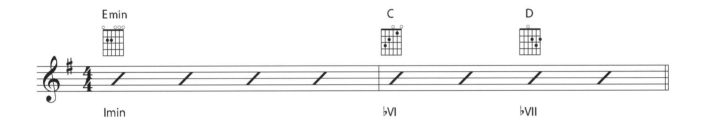

Listen

Listen to this example based on that same minor-key progression. Notice that in this variation, the *last* chord is subtracted.

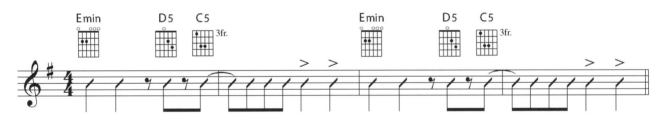

Listen again, and play along with the recording. The power chords give it an edgier sound.

Writing Exercises

Complete at least one of these exercises. Play and practice it along with one of the drum tracks, or create your own rhythm groove. Use any of the rhythmic tools from unit I to generate your grooves.

■ Practice

Create a groove by subtracting one of the chords from the "Imin IImin ♭III IImin" progression or from any progression of your choice.

■ Rewrite the Hits

Choose a progression from a song you know (or a song mentioned in this lesson). Subtract one of the chords from the original progression to transform it into something original.

■ Create Your Own Melody

Transform any progression you know by subtracting one of the chords, and then create your own melody to go with it.

■ Write a Song

Create a song section, with melody and lyrics, on a chord progression that you've varied by subtracting chords.

LESSON 31
Add Chords

Adding chords to a common progression can produce a lot of distinctive new versions of it.

Hit songs created by adding a new chord to a common progression include "Takin' Care of Business" [C], "Saturday Night's Alright" [G Mixolydian], "Centerfold" [G Mixolydian], "Spirits in the Material World" [Amin], "Can't Stand Losin' You" [Dmin], "Lay Down Sally" [A blues], "Old Time Rock and Roll" [G♭], "Every Breath You Take" [G], "Stand By Me" [F], and many others.

You can add chords in one of two ways: adding original chords and adding chords from outside the progression.

Adding Original Chords

You can add chords that come from the progression itself, inserting them at new places within the progression. Consider the common power progression "I IV V."

Original

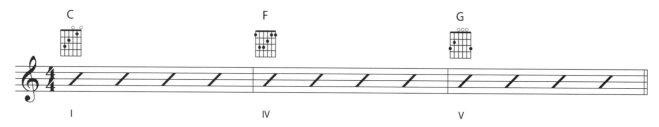

Here are three variations of that progression. They were created by adding one of the progression's original chords back into it, in a new place. Also listed are some hit songs based on each variation.

Variation 1. I IV V IV
"Hang On Sloopy," "Louie Louie," "Twist and Shout," "Walking on Sunshine," "La Bamba," "Get Off of My Cloud," "Piece of My Heart," "Wild Thing"

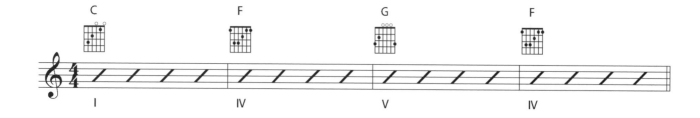

Variation 2. I IV V I
"Only the Good Die Young," "Lay Down Sally," "Old Time Rock and Roll"

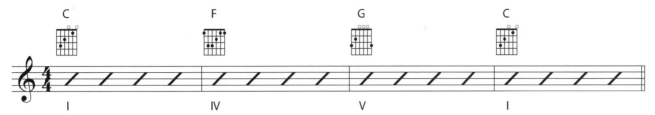

Variation 3. I V IV V
"Jack and Diane"

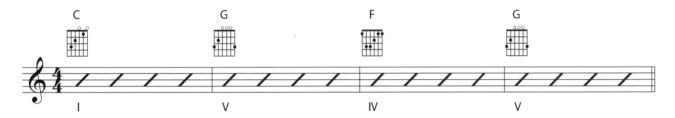

Adding Outside Chords

You can also add chords that come from outside the progression—either in or out of the progression's key. Again, we'll start with the power progression "I IV V."

Original

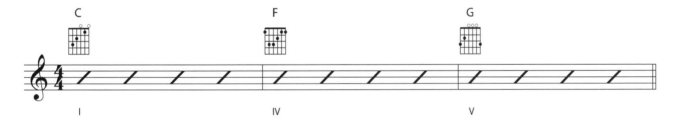

The following progressions were created by adding new chords to this common progression. Some of the hits based on them are listed. Notice that these variations also use different phrase lengths or other rhythm variations.

By adding IIImin, we get the progression used in "I Feel Fine."

Variation 4. I IIImin IV V

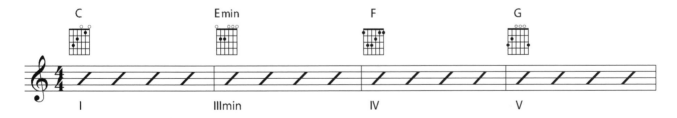

By adding VImin, we get the progression used in tunes such as "Hit Me with Your Best Shot," "She Drives Me Crazy," "More Than a Feeling," "I'm Goin' Down," "So Lonely," "Hurts So Good," and many others.

Variation 5. I IV VImin V

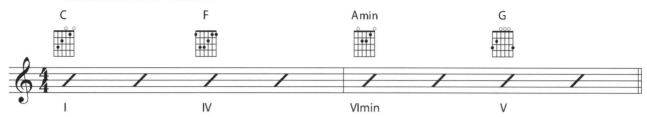

Listen

Listen to this example, based on variation 5 above. Notice that a chord outside the key, ♭VII, is added to the end of the progression, adding a bluesy color, and making the progression longer. Then listen again, and play along with the recording.

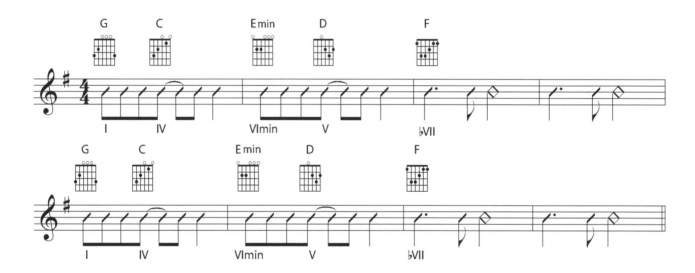

Writing Exercises

80 to 85

Complete at least one of these exercises. Play and practice it along with one of the drum tracks, or create your own rhythm groove. Use any of the rhythmic tools from unit I to generate your grooves.

■ Practice

Create a groove by adding an original chord or a new chord into the "I IV V" progression or any common progression of your choice.

■ Rewrite the Hits

Choose a progression from a song you know (or a song mentioned in this lesson). Add a new chord to this progression to transform it into something original.

■ Create Your Own Melody

Transform any progression you know by adding one or more chords, and then create your own melody to go with it.

■ Write a Song

Create a song with melody and lyrics, on a chord progression that you've varied by adding chords.

LESSON 32
Replace Chords

Replacing chord(s) in a progression can produce a fresh version of that progression.

Hit songs created by replacing a chord in a common progression include "Heartache Tonight" [G], "Fantasy" [C], "Salisbury Hill" [D], "Just My Imagination" [G], "Dreamlover" [C], "Best of My Love" [C], "September" [A], "I'll Have to Say I Love You in a Song" [A], "Let's Get It On" [Eb], "My Girl" [F], "I've Got Love on My Mind" [D], "Hungry for You" [C], "Midnight Train to Georgia" [F], "Piano Man" [C], "Mister Bojangles" [D], "When a Man Loves a Woman" [D], "Hello, Goodbye" [C], "The Closer I Get to You" [A], and many others.

Take a progression and simply substitute another chord you choose for one or more of the original chords. You can substitute a chord *in* or *out* of the key.

Here is a common power progression: "I VImin IV V."

Original

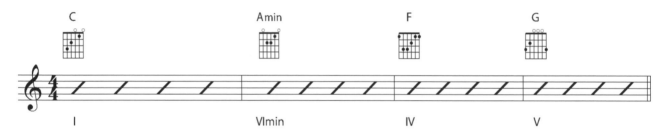

By replacing a chord, we can create many variations. Here are a few, with some hits that were based on them. Notice that many use additional rhythmic and pitch variation techniques as well.

Variation 1
Replace VImin with IIImin7, which results in the chord progression used in "Let's Get It On," "I've Got Love on My Mind," and "Midnight Train to Georgia."

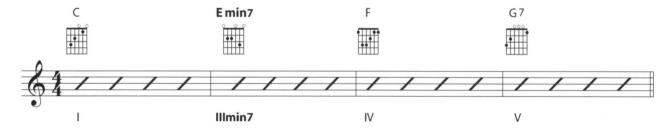

Variation 2

Replace VImin with IImin, which results in the chord progression used in "My Girl," "Hungry for You," and "Love Is All Around."

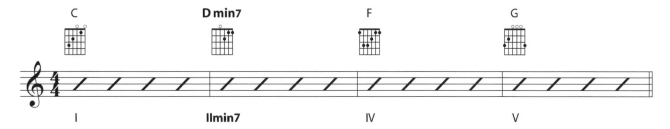

Variation 3

Replace two chords: VImin and IV with IIImin7 and IImin7, which is the progression used in "I'll Have to Say I Love You in a Song."

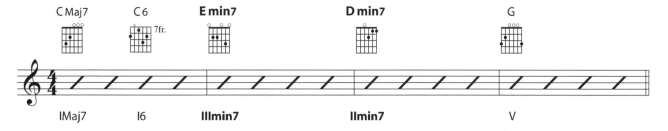

Here is another common power progression: the descending "I I/7 VImin I/5 IV I/3 IImin V." (Note: All progressions are presented in the key of C major.)

Original

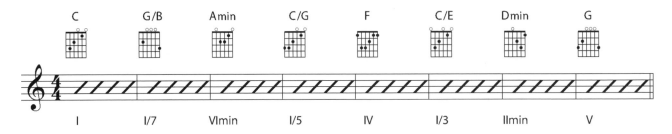

These variations have yielded grooves in the styles of the listed hits, and many others.

Variation 1
"Piano Man"

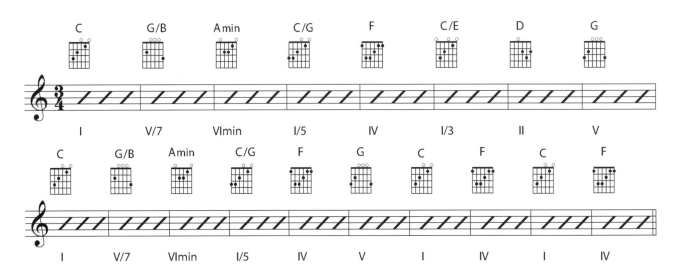

Variation 2
"Mister Bojangles"

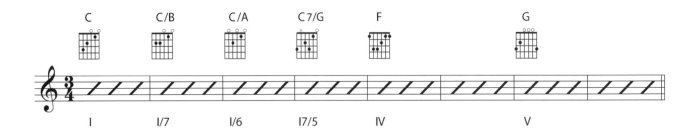

Variation 3
"When a Man Loves a Woman"

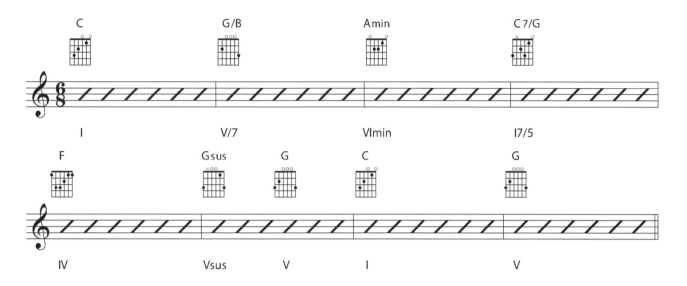

Variation 4
"Three Times a Lady"

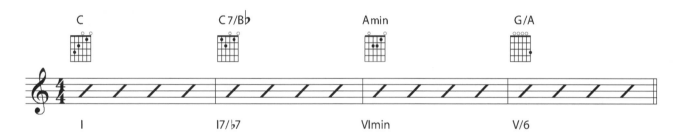

Variation 5
"Together Again"

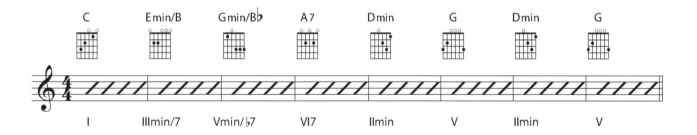

Variation 6
"Hello, Goodbye"

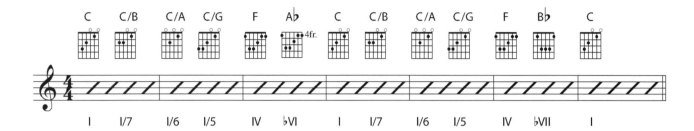

C	C/B	C/A	C/G	F	A♭	C	C/B	C/A	C/G	F	B♭	C
I	I/7	I/6	I/5	IV	♭VI	I	I/7	I/6	I/5	IV	♭VII	I

Variation 7
"Can't Let Go"

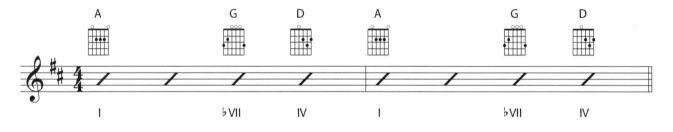

C	C/B	B♭	F/A	G/B
I	I/7	♭VII	IV/6	V/7

Listen

Listen to this example based on the variation of the Mixolydian progression "I ♭VII IV." The V major chord (V7sus4), from out of the key, replaces the IV chord and brings in a brighter color.

Original

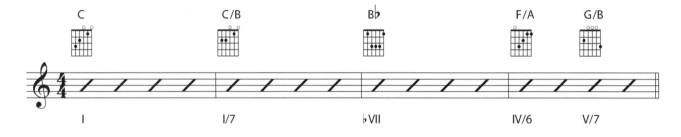

A	G	D	A	G	D
I	♭VII	IV	I	♭VII	IV

Variation

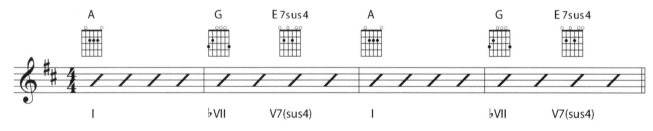

A	G	E7sus4	A	G	E7sus4
I	♭VII	V7(sus4)	I	♭VII	V7(sus4)

Listen again, and play along with the recording. Notice that the phrase length of the variation is two measures long, rather than just one.

Writing Exercises

Complete at least one of these exercises. Play and practice it along with one of the drum tracks, or create your own rhythm groove. Use any of the rhythmic tools from unit I to generate your grooves.

■ Practice

Create a groove by replacing a chord in any of the progressions from this lesson or any progression of your choice.

■ Rewrite the Hits

Choose a progression from a song you know (or a song mentioned in this lesson). Replace one or more chords in the original progression to transform it into something original.

■ Create Your Own Melody

Transform any progression you know by replacing one or more chords, and then create your own melody to go with it.

■ Write a Song

Create a song with melody and lyrics, on a chord progression that you've varied by replacing chords.

LESSON 33
Add a Pedal

A *pedal* is a short, repeating melodic idea. It can be in either the bass or another instrument. Adding a pedal is another way to create your own version of a chord progression. Pedals can help make a progression sound more modern.

Hit songs using pedals include "I Still Haven't Found What I'm Looking For" [D], "You and I" [F], "Boogie On Reggae Woman" [A♭ Mixolydian], "I Can See for Miles" [E], "Billie Jean" [F♯ Dorian], "Only You Know and I Know" [E♭ Mixolydian], "Sweet Emotion" [A], "Up Where We Belong" [D], "Hollywood Nights" [E Mixolydian], "Gimme Some Lovin'" [E], and many others.

There are two ways to add pedals. You can add:

1. the tonic note

2. a short, repeating melodic idea (called an "ostinato")

Listen

Listen to this progression and three variations. Notice the three different ways you can vary any progression by adding a pedal. These pedal variations are based on the power progression "I ♭III IV" (A C D).

Original

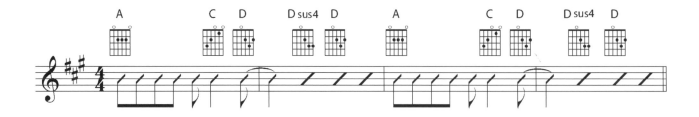

Variation 1
Add a single-note pedal (on the tonic note, A) in the bass.

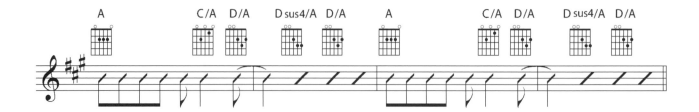

Variation 2

Add a melodic pedal part in the bass.

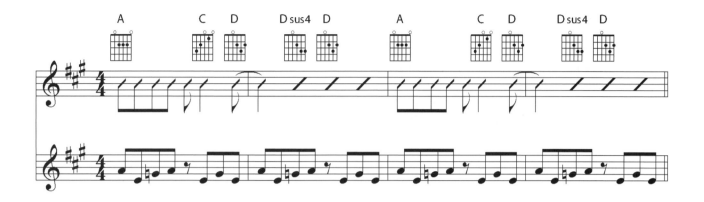

Variation 3

Add a melodic pedal part in another instrument, besides the bass.

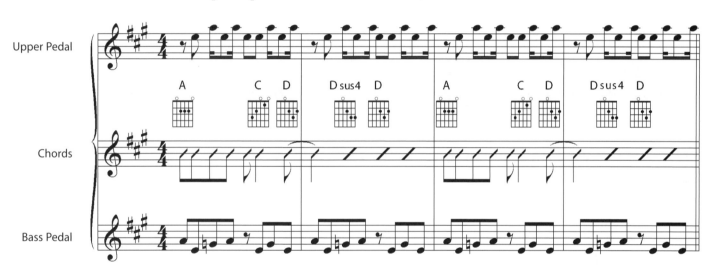

Listen again, and play along with the recording. Notice how each version sounds a little different, and all make the progression sound a little more modern.

Writing Exercises

Complete at least one of these exercises. Play and practice it along with one of the drum tracks, or create your own rhythm groove. Use any of the rhythmic tools from unit I to generate your grooves.

Add pedals parts in each of the three ways described in this lesson:

1. Add a one-note bass pedal, using the tonic note.

2. Add a melodic bass pedal.

3. Add a melodic pedal in another instrument, besides bass.

■ Practice

Create a groove by adding a pedal part into the "I ♭III IV" progression or any progression of your choice.

■ Rewrite the Hits

Choose a progression from a song you know (or a song mentioned in this lesson). Create three variations of it by adding each of the three types of pedals. Which one works best?

■ Create Your Own Melody

Transform any progression you know by adding pedals, and create your own melody to go with it.

■ Write a Song

Create a song, with melody and lyrics, on a chord progression that you've varied by adding a pedal.

B. Building Song Sections

The tools for pitch variations of progressions can all be used to create song sections that fit together organically, as well as sound continually fresh and interesting.

In part B, you will learn some of the ways to use these tools to create song sections that work well together.

LESSON 34

Pitch Contrast: Two Sections from One Progression

You can create two contrasting sections based on the same chord progression by using different pitch variation techniques in each section. As with the tools for rhythmic contrast, this creates a unity between the sections, while keeping each one interesting and distinct.

Hit songs that use pitch variations on progressions between two sections include "She Loves You" [G], "Tracks of My Tears" [G], and many others.

In tunes such as "She Loves You," the different sections may include pitch variations of the power progression "I VImin IV V." Here, in both the verse and the chorus, the IV chord is replaced. The verse substitutes the IIImin chord, which comes from within the key. The chorus substitutes the IVmin chord, which comes from outside the key.

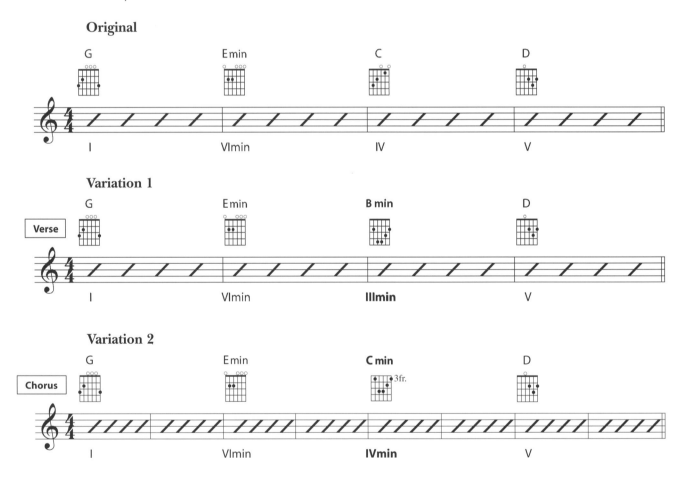

Notice other important tools for contrasting sections:

■ contrast chords *in* the key with chords *out* of the key

■ contrast the progressions' *lengths*

■ contrast the chords' *rhythm* (verse: 1 measure/chord, chorus: 2 measures/chord)

Listen

Listen to this next example, and notice the two versions of the "I7 IV7" blues progression. (Chords in **bold type** come from outside the key.)

Verse (original): I7 IV7 (A7 D7)
Chorus: I ♭**III** IV ♭**VI** ♭**VII** (A5 **C5** D5 **F5** **G5**)

Listen again, and play along with the recording. Notice that the chorus has a different phrase length. Also, notice the contrast gained by substituting a chord in the key, for the verse, and one out of the key in the chorus. How is the melody different in the verse and chorus?

Writing Exercises

Complete at least one of these exercises. Play and practice it along with one of the drum tracks, or create your own rhythm groove. Use any of the rhythmic tools from unit I to generate your grooves.

Try combining the pitch variations with the rhythm variations you learned in unit IV.

■ Practice

Create two contrasting sections using two different pitch variations of the same progression. Replace, add, or subtract chords from any progression of your choice.

■ Rewrite the Hits

Choose a progression from any song you know (or a song mentioned in this lesson). Replace, add, or subtract chords from this progression to create two contrasting sections, based on it.

■ Create Your Own Melody

Complete the "Practice" or "Rewrite the Hits" exercise above. Then, create your own melody to go with it.

■ Write a Song

Complete the "Create Your Own Melody" exercise above, and add lyrics.

LESSON 35
Three Contrasting Sections from One Progression

You can also create three contrasting sections incorporating rhythmic and pitch variations of the same progression. This can help *you create a whole song from different versions of the same chord progression.*

Hit songs with three contrasting sections, all based on the same progression, include "Gimme Some Lovin'" [E], "How Will I Know" [G♭], and many others.

Some tunes use different variations of a power progression in each section. For example, the tune "Gimme Some Lovin'" is based on a "I IV" power progression.

Original: I IV

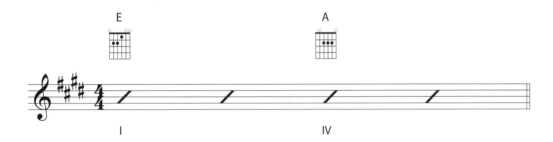

It uses different variations of this progression in the verse, prechorus, and chorus.

Variation 1

Variation 2

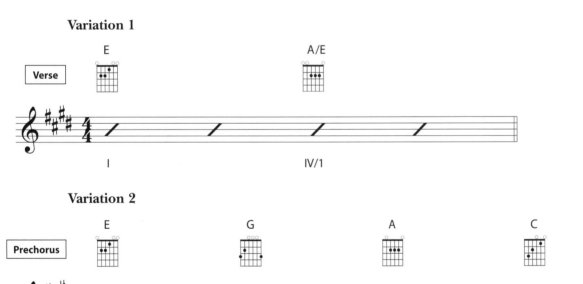

Variation 3

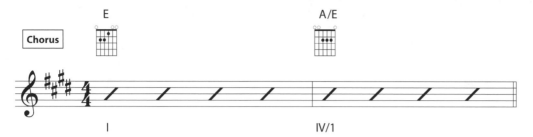

Notice the other important tools used for contrasting these sections:

- A pedal (verse, chorus) vs. a standard bass part (prechorus).

- The length of the progressions (verse: 1 bar, prechorus: 4 bars, chorus: 2 bars).

- The shape or direction of the bass line. The bass pedal in the verse and chorus contrasts with the ascending bass line in the prechorus.

Listen

Listen to the following example that uses three different pitch variations of the progression "I ♭III ♭VII," used in tunes such as "Ohio" and "Cover Me."

Listen again, and play along with the recording. Notice that the chorus melody is based on the bass line. *Singing the title to the bass melody helps to emphasize title.* (For more on this technique, see *The Songwriter's Workshop: Melody.*)

Writing Exercises

Complete at least one of these exercises. Play and practice it along with one of the drum tracks, or create your own rhythm groove. Use any of the rhythmic tools from unit I to generate your grooves. Try combining the pitch variations with the rhythm variations you learned in unit IV.

■ Practice

Create a verse, prechorus, and chorus using different pitch and/or rhythm variations of the same progression.

■ Rewrite the Hits

Choose a progression from a song you know (or a song mentioned in this lesson). Create a verse, prechorus, and chorus using different pitch and/or rhythm variations of that progression.

■ Create Your Own Melody

Complete either the "Practice" or "Rewrite the Hits" exercises above, and add a melody to go with it.

■ Write a Song

Complete the "Create Your Own Melody" exercise above, and add lyrics.

UNIT VII
Harmony and Melody

So far, the approach we've taken is to begin the songwriting process with the groove and the chord progression, which can be modified and customized as you develop the melody and lyrics. This is the most common way that songwriters work, but there are other approaches, too.

Now, we will approach the songwriting process in the opposite way: beginning with the melody and lyrics, and then developing harmony to support them.

In practice, you will use a combination of these different approaches, switching between them throughout the process. Being able to work in either way will help you to overcome writer's block.

A. Harmonizing Melody Notes

When working with an existing melodic or lyrical idea, you will develop the song's harmony by creating chords to color a word, or to color a melodic phrase. In this way, you can create very specific expressive effects, at specific locations in your song.

LESSON 36
Coloring a Word

A chord's color can affect the meaning and impact of a lyric, especially when the critical word comes at the end of a phrase. When a lyric's meaning is ambiguous, the chord color will influence how that lyric is understood.

Hit songs that use harmonies to color the specific meanings of lyrics include "Still Crazy after All These Years" [C], "Just the Way You Are" [D], "The Sounds of Silence" [Amin], "Nothing Compares to You" [F], and many others.

Listen

Listen to how the word "love" can have different meanings, depending on its accompanying harmony. How does the meaning change, as the harmonizations move through major chords, power chords, minor chords, and seventh chords? Notice that *the emotional color and meaning of the word change in spite of the fact that the melody note is always the same.* These meanings might be described as:

- Major: hopeful, positive

- Power: powerful, assertive

- Minor: sad, introspective

- Seventh: bluesy, sexy

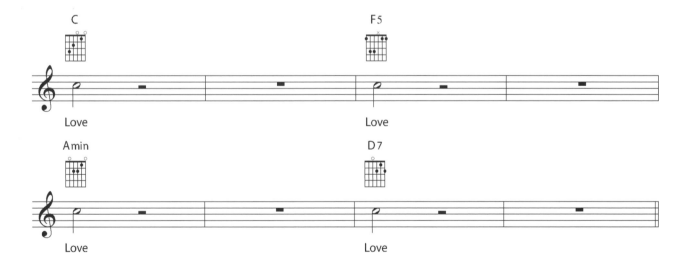

Even within each chord color, the same word can have subtly different meanings. Listen to all the different emotional tones of the same word on all four chord colors.

Major Chord Color

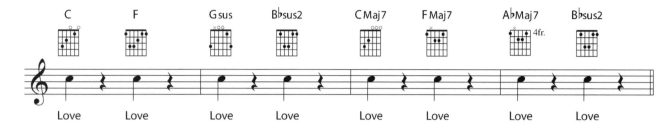

Power Chord Color

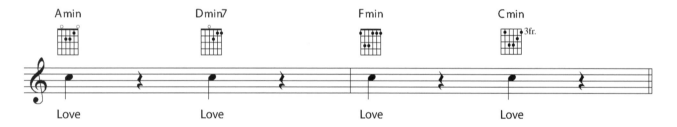

Minor Chord Color

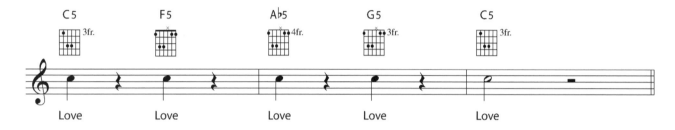

Seventh Chord Color

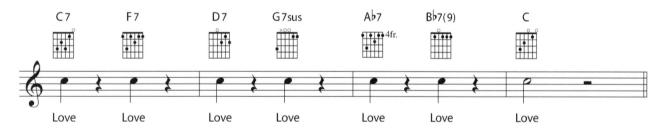

Listen again, and play/sing along with the recording. Notice how the chords all subtly affect the meaning of the same word, even within the same chord color.

Writing Exercises

Complete at least one of these exercises. Play and practice it along with "Heart (no chords)," or create your own rhythm groove. Use any of the rhythmic tools from unit I to generate your grooves.

■ Practice

Sing the word "Heart" on the note C, against all the chords in this lesson (or any other chords you know). Then choose one of these settings, and create a groove for "Heart" based on it.

Heart   Heart   Heart   Heart   Heart   Heart   Heart   Heart

■ Rewrite the Hits

Choose any song you know (or one mentioned in this lesson) that includes a word that can have many meanings. Sing that word on the note C. Set it to as many chords as you can, and see how they change its meaning.

■ Create Your Own Melody

Choose any word that can have many meanings, and sing it on the note C. Set it to as many chords as you can, and see how they change its meaning.

■ Write a Song

Create a song section with a lyric centered around one note. Change the emotional meaning of that word by setting it against many different chord colors.

LESSON 37
Coloring a Phrase

In the same way that a single chord can change the feeling of a single word, a progression of two or more chords can change the feeling of an entire lyric/melodic phrase. This lesson will show you how to color a phrase by using different chord progressions.

Hit songs that distinguish a phrase by using a chord progression include "Still Crazy after All These Years" [C], "Just the Way You Are" [D], "The Sound of Silence" [Amin], "Nothing Compares to You" [F], and many others.

Listen

 Listen to the lyric phrase "I Learned a Lot about Love" (melody only, without any harmony). In the key of C, it ends on the tonic note, C.

Original

I   Learned   a   Lot   a - bout   Love.

Ending a melody on the tonic gives the phrase a "resolved" emotional feeling. In this case, the singer is making a positive statement about the good things they've learned about love. But as we discussed in the previous lesson, the chord you put under "love" can change that.

Let's say that you want to write a song where "love" isn't necessarily happy and positive. You may want it to be longing, or ironic, or angry. One way to do this is by changing the chords.

This lyric phrase has two essential notes in the melody, D and C. To recolor the phrase, list the different chords that you might want to try under each. You might create a chart with two columns, showing the different possible chord choices for each note. There are different ways to organize this, but let's have one column for measure 1, and one for measure 2.

Which chord color works best for each part of the phrase? Try different chords, and practice the whole phrase together, as well as each part by itself. You can also try using two chords in the same measure, to create a little motion (as in variations 3 and 4, coming up).

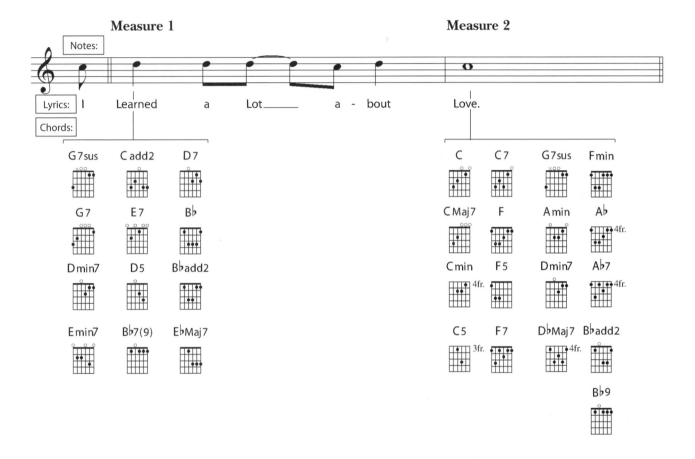

Listen to some ways of reharmonizing this phrase. Again, notice how the emotional color and meaning of the whole phrase changes in spite of the fact that the melody note is always the same. Then listen again, and play along with the recording. After each repetition of the phrase, stop the recording, and write down what you think the "story" of the song will be about.

Writing Exercises

Complete at least one of these exercises. Play and practice it along with "Melody Phrase Only." Use any of the rhythmic tools from unit I to generate your grooves. Try the exercise a number of times, and consider what the "story" of each solution might be about.

■ Practice

Create a 2-chord progression to accompany the "I learned a lot about love" lyric, choosing one chord from column 1 and one chord from column 2 (see the chart, earlier this lesson). You can even experiment, creating a 2-chord progression under the first measure.

■ Rewrite the Hits

Choose a simple phrase, preferably using two notes, from a song you know (or one mentioned in this lesson). Harmonize each note with as many different chords as you can. Then create as many harmonizations of that phrase as you can.

■ Create Your Own Melody

Write a phrase of your own that centers around two notes. Find as many chords as you can to harmonize each note. Then create as many harmonizations of that phrase as you can.

■ Write a Song

Create a chorus with a lyric and melodic phrase that repeats four times. Then reharmonize the melody to change the meaning of the chorus.

B. Building Sections

In this part, you will control the meaning of a whole lyric section by the chords you choose.

LESSON 38
Coloring a Lyric Section

Trying different ways of harmonizing a song section can help you find the best way to reflect a lyric's meaning.

Hit songs that color entire lyric sections through chord progressions include "Sound of Silence" [Amin], "Still Crazy After All These Years" [C], "She's Always a Woman to Me" [E♭], "You and I" [F], "Blowin' in the Wind" [D], "Barracuda" [E Blues], "Savin' All My Love for You" [A], "It's Still Rock 'n' Roll to Me" [C], "Just the Way You Are" [D], and many others.

Listen

Listen to "I Learned a Lot about Love (no chords)." Notice how the lyrics can be interpreted in many different ways. The chords under each measure are some of the many choices to color words and notes in that measure. Try playing and singing different chords, focusing on the unique feelings that each setting brings out.

Original

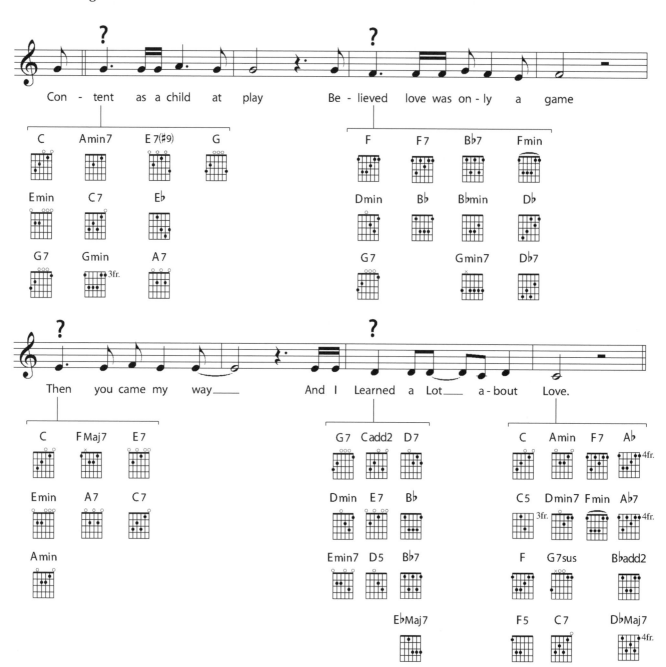

Now, you'll hear two different reharmonizations of this tune. Listen to the first variation, and then pause the recording. What kind of story does it suggest to you?

Variation 1

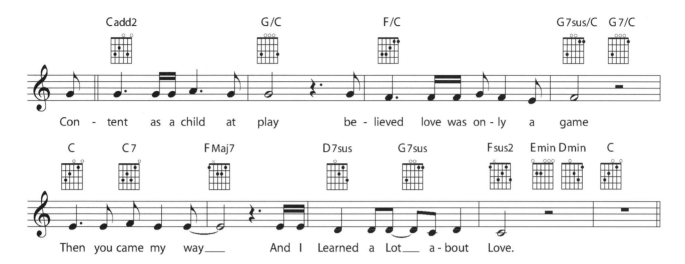

Con - tent as a child at play be - lieved love was on - ly a game

Then you came my way___ And I Learned a Lot___ a - bout Love.

Now, listen to the second harmonization. What kind of story does this one tell? How does the harmony reflect a different emotion?

Variation 2

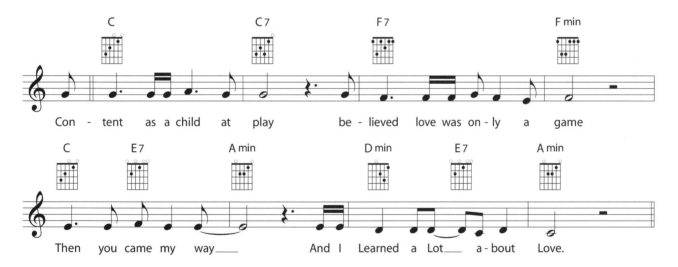

Con - tent as a child at play be - lieved love was on - ly a game

Then you came my way___ And I Learned a Lot___ a - bout Love.

Using Reharmonization

As you become more familiar with different types of chords, you will find it easier to match chords with lyric meaning. If you are not sure which chord to use, look at the melody note, and list a number of different chords that include that melody note in them. Then try them all. Start with basic chord colors first, and then try adding notes, to customize them to your specific lyric.

Writing Exercises

Complete at least one of these exercises. Play and practice it along with "Melody Phrase Only," or create your own rhythm groove. Use any of the rhythmic tools from unit I to generate your grooves.

■ Practice

Listen to the vocal track "Verse/Refrain (no chords)" (CD 56). What feeling do you get from these lyrics?

Choose one chord from each measure of the examples in this lesson. Then use these chords to harmonize the vocal track. Remember, you can use two chords in some measures.

■ Rewrite the Hits

Choose a simple melody from any song you know (or a song mentioned in this lesson).

1. First, try replacing some of the original chords.

2. Then replace all the chords.

How many ways can you use chords to change the lyric's meaning?

■ Create Your Own Melody

Create your own melody. Find as many chords as you can to color its various notes. Then create as many versions of it as you can. Note the emotional feeling of each, and decide which one best reflects the lyric's story.

■ Write a Song

Create melodies and lyrics for two contrasting sections. Create as many chord versions of each section as you can. Note the emotional feeling of each, and decide which one best reflects the lyric's story.

UNIT VIII
Home and Away

In harmony, the tonic chord can be thought of as "home." It is resolved, and the song's harmonic tension is released. All other chords are considered "away from home" and unresolved, especially when they are set at the end of lyric phrases and the end of song sections.

In this unit, you will learn about some of the harmonic journeys you can take, bringing the song home to the tonic, or to some of the other places you can go.

A. Harmonic Journeys

The power progressions generally begin on the tonic (home) and end on another chord (away). These progressions, and others, are called *repetitive* progressions because they tend to repeat over and over, throughout a section.

Another type of chord progression is called a *through-composed* progression. These tend not to repeat, and will span an entire song section.

A third type of chord motion is the *cadence*—a chord change between a "home" chord and an "away" chord. Cadences are the strongest type of harmonic motion. In part A of this unit, we explore the five most important cadences: four that "come home" in different ways, and one that "stays away."

LESSON 39
Full Cadences

The *full cadence* is the strongest motion from "away" to "home." It begins on one of the chords farthest removed from the tonic and then moves to the tonic (such as V to I, in major). Because this is such a strong motion, full cadences are often chosen as settings for the title.

Full cadences are common in all key colors except Dorian. We will look at full cadences in each of the other key colors individually.

1. Major-Key Full Cadences

Hit songs in major that set the title to a full cadence include "Fields of Gold" [D], "I Want to Hold Your Hand" [G], "Everybody Plays the Fool" [Bb], "How Sweet It Is" [G], "Time after Time" [C], "Tracks of My Tears" [G], "Heat Wave" [D], "Blowin' in the Wind" [D], "Just the Way You Are" [D], "The Times They Are A-Changin'" [D], "It's Still Rock and Roll to Me" [C], "I Just Called to Say I Love You" [Db], "Straight from the Heart" [A], and many others.

Listen

The simplest full cadence in major goes from V to I [G7 to C]. Listen to this example, in which a simple "V7 I" full cadence is followed by other common variations, either adding or replacing chords in the original. Notice how they all sound resolved when they end on the I chord.

Listen again, and play along with the recording. Notice that the cadences are of different lengths, and that they each reflect the resolved emotion of the title.

Setting your title to a full cadence is one of the strongest ways to emphasize it. When the lyric ends on the I chord, the cadence brings the point "home" to the audience. *Remember, this will be effective only if the lyric is about a resolved emotion.* It can be used in any song form.

2. Minor Full Cadences

Hit songs in minor that set the title to a full cadence include "Emotions" [Amin], "Rock and Roll Hoochie Koo" [Amin], "Easy Lover" [Fmin], "Russians" [Cmin], and many others.

The most common minor-key full cadence is ♭VII to Imin [G to Amin]. Occasionally, you will find V to Imin [E to Amin or Emin to Amin]. Listen to this example, in which a "♭VII Imin" full cadence is followed by other common variations. Notice how they all sound resolved when they end on the Imin chord. This example is in A minor.

If your song is in a minor key, you can set your title to any of these full cadences. It will give a very somber feel to the lyric.

3. Blues Full Cadences

Hit songs in blues keys that set the title to a full cadence include "I Feel Fine" [G], "Respect" [C], "The Midnight Hour" [E♭], and many others.

 The blues cadence comes from the last four measures of the 12-bar blues. Listen to this example of the standard blues full cadence.

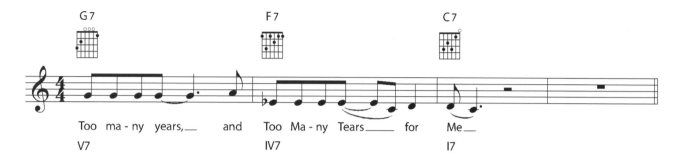

4. Mixolydian Full Cadences

Hit songs in Mixolydian that set the title line to a full cadence include: "Help" [A], "Reelin' in the Years" [A].

 The Mixolydian cadence goes from ♭VII to I. Listen to this example of a typical Mixolydian cadence.

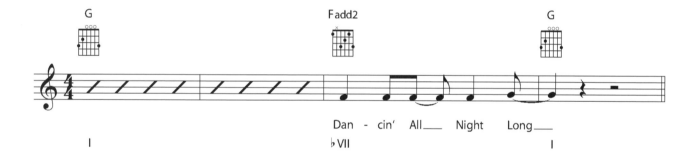

Writing Exercises

 to

Complete at least one of these exercises. Play and practice it along with one of the drum tracks, or create your own rhythm groove. Use any of the rhythmic tools from unit I to generate your grooves.

■ Practice

Create a full cadence in several key colors.

■ Rewrite the Hits

Choose a progression from a song you know (or one mentioned in this lesson) that sets the title over a full cadence. Then reset this title over a different full cadence.

■ Create Your Own Melody

Choose an original title that describes a resolved emotion. Set it to a melody that ends in a full cadence. Notice how the cadence affects your title's meaning.

■ Write a Song

Create a title lyric that describes a definite, resolved emotion. Write a song section that includes this title. Then set this section to music. When the title occurs, set it to a full cadence.

LESSON 40
Half Cadences

The *half cadence* is a progression that ends "away" on the V chord (G7 in C major, Emin in A minor). It doesn't come home at all. It is used to build tension. At the end of a verse, a half cadence will help to set up the chorus (as we will see in part B of this unit).

Hit songs that use half cadences include "Nothing Compares to You" [F], "She's Gone" [E♭], "How Am I Supposed to Live Without You?" [B♭], "Reason to Believe" [G], "Paint It Black" [Fmin], and many others.

Half cadences are usually used in major keys, and only occasionally in other keys.

Listen

 Listen to this example, which has a chord progression that ends with a half cadence to G, the V chord of C. Notice how ending on the V sounds unresolved.

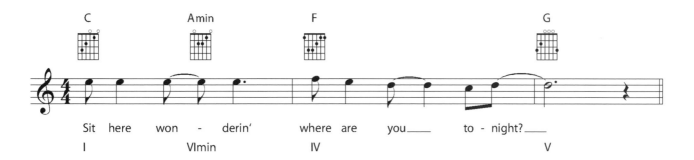

Listen again, and play along with the recording. In addition to the unresolved V chord, notice that the melody ends on a note (D) that isn't the tonic (C). This adds to the unresolved feeling of the lyric. Half cadences are an effective way to set your title when the lyric is about an unresolved emotion, and you can use it in any song form.

Writing Exercises

Complete at least one of these exercises. Play and practice it along with one of the drum tracks, or create your own rhythm groove. Use any of the rhythmic tools from unit I to generate your grooves.

■ Practice

Create a chord progression that ends in a half cadence (either major or minor).

■ Rewrite the Hits

Choose a progression from any song you know (or one mentioned in this lesson) that sets the title line over a half cadence. Then reset this title over a different half cadence.

■ Create Your Own Melody

Choose an original title that describes an unresolved emotion. Set it to a melody that ends in a half cadence. Avoid singing the tonic at the end of the title. Notice how the cadence affects your title's meaning.

■ Write a Song

Create a lyric that describes an indefinite, unresolved emotion, and contains the title. Set it to music, and when the title occurs, set it to a half cadence.

LESSON 41
Deceptive Cadences

The *deceptive cadence* is a progression that comes to a point of resolution that is not the tonic. This adds an element of surprise to the progression. It sounds resolved, but much less than the full cadence. In this lesson you'll learn the effect of deceptive cadences on the lyric. You'll use them to move from a verse to a chorus in part B.

Hit songs that set the title to a deceptive cadence include: "Fields of Gold" [D], "Still Crazy after All These Years" [C], "Every Breath You Take" [E♭], "With or Without You" [D], "New York State of Mind" [C], and many others.

Deceptive cadences are usually used in major, and occasionally, in minor keys.

The deceptive cadence is when the V chord resolves to a chord that isn't the I chord. The most common deceptive cadence is when V goes to VI minor [G7 to A minor, in C].

Listen

Listen to these examples of some common deceptive cadences. In order, they go to the VImin (Amin), IV (F), and VI major (A) chords. Notice how each affects the meaning of the lyric.

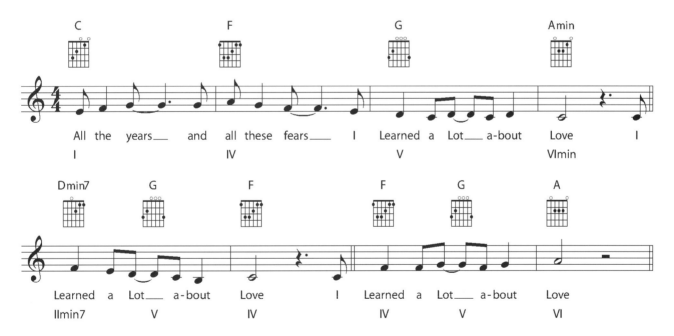

Listen again, and play along with the recording. How would you describe the different meanings of the different lyric settings? Most listeners would describe the first as sorrowful, the second as a positive surprise, and the third as a bright, happy surprise. Each says something different about what the songwriter learned about love.

Setting your title to the deceptive cadence is especially useful when the title's meaning is emotionally ambiguous. You can use it in any song form.

Writing Exercises

80 to 85 Complete at least one of these exercises. Play and practice it along with one of the drum tracks, or create your own rhythm groove. Use any of the rhythmic tools from unit I to generate your grooves.

■ Practice

Create a chord progression that ends in a deceptive cadence in any major key.

■ Rewrite the Hits

Choose a progression from a song you know (or one mentioned in this lesson) that sets the title line over a deceptive cadence. Then reset this title over a different deceptive cadence.

■ Create Your Own Melody

Choose an original title. Set it to a melody three times, beginning each time on the V chord and ending first on the VI minor, then on the IV major, and then on the VI major chords. Notice the effect of each ending on the meaning of your title.

■ Write a Song

Create a lyric that describes an indefinite, unresolved, emotion, and contains the title line. Set it to music, and when the title occurs, set it to a deceptive cadence.

LESSON 42
Plagal Cadences

The plagal (or "amen") cadence moves from IV to I, coming home in a subtler way than the full cadence does. It is the usual setting for the lyric "amen" at the end of hymns.

Hit songs using some version of the plagal cadence include "Tracks of My Tears" [G], "Let It Be" [C], "Yesterday" [F], "Candle in the Wind" [A], "Eight Days a Week" [D], "Strawberry Fields Forever" [A], "A Whiter Shade of Pale" [C], "Lean on Me" [C], "The Way You Do Things You Do" [G], and many others.

Plagal cadences are most common in major keys.

Listen

Listen to these examples of some common plagal cadences. The first one is the simplest: it goes from IV to I. The others substitute other chords but have similar effects. Notice how they all affect the meaning of the lyric.

Listen again, and play along with the recording. How would you describe the meanings of the lyrics? Most listeners would describe them as having a religious or spiritual emotion. This probably comes from the "amen" heritage. Setting a title across a plagal cadence recalls this emotion. It can be used in any song form.

Writing Exercises

Complete at least one of these exercises. Play and practice it along with one of the drum tracks, or create your own rhythm groove. Use any of the rhythmic tools from unit I to generate your grooves.

■ Practice

Create a chord progression that ends in a plagal cadence in any major key.

■ Rewrite the Hits

Choose a progression from a song you know (or one mentioned in this lesson) that sets the title line over a plagal cadence. Then reset this title over a different plagal cadence.

■ Create Your Own Melody

Set an original title to a melody across a plagal cadence. Notice how the cadence affects your title's meaning.

■ Write a Song

Create a lyric that has an inspirational, spiritual, or religious theme, and contains the title. Set it to music, and when the title occurs, set it to a plagal cadence.

LESSON 43
Mixed Cadences

Mixed cadences use chords from keys of a different key color, but on the same tonic. They often use minor-key chords in a major key.

Hit songs using a mixed cadence include "Brown Sugar" [C], "Lady Madonna" [A], "I Can See for Miles" [E], and many others.

Mixed cadences are most common in major keys.

Listen

Listen to these examples of some common mixed cadences. The first one is the simplest: it uses the "♭VI ♭VII Imin" cadence from minor, but set in a major key. The next one mixes the ♭VII chord from a Mixolydian key with the regular "V I" full cadence. Notice how each affects the meaning of the lyric.

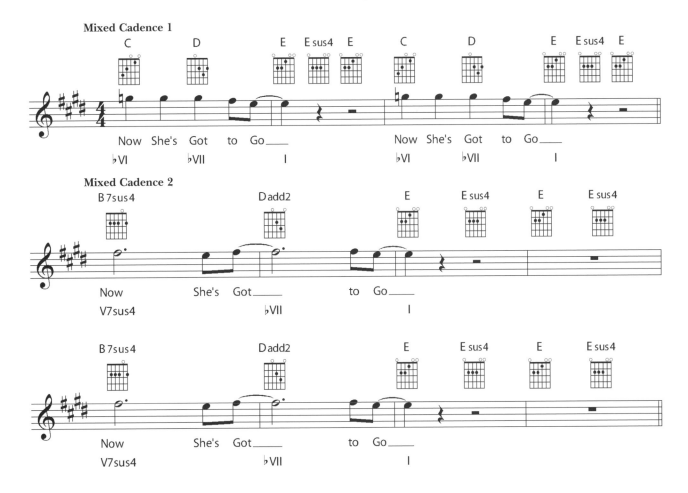

Listen again, and play along with the recording. How would you describe the meanings of the lyrics? Most listeners describe them as having a mixture of the sad emotions of minor and the more positive emotions of major.

Setting your title across the chords of a mixed cadence is particularly useful in songs that mix sad and happy feelings, especially in rock- or blues-based songs. It works in any song form.

Writing Exercises

Complete at least one of these exercises. Play and practice it along with one of the drum tracks, or create your own rhythm groove. Use any of the rhythmic tools from unit I to generate your grooves.

■ Practice

Create a chord progression that ends in a mixed cadence, using minor cadence chords in a major key.

■ Rewrite the Hits

Choose a progression from a song you know (or one mentioned in this lesson) that sets the title line over a mixed cadence. Then reset this title over a different mixed cadence.

■ Create Your Own Melody

Choose an original title, and set it to a melody across a mixed cadence. Notice how the cadence affects your title's meaning.

■ Write a Song

Create a lyric that mixes emotions or has a rock/blues feeling. Set it to music in a major key, and when the title occurs, set it to a mixed cadence.

B. Building Song Sections

Cadences are especially useful in connecting two song sections. Part B shows how to use them in this way, strengthening the feelings of "home" and "away," and using that to intensify the meaning of your lyrics.

LESSON 44
Verse/Refrain: Home/Away/Home

A verse that contains the title is sometimes called a *verse/refrain*. Cadences are commonly used to emphasize the title line, in these song structures.

Hit songs using cadences in verse/refrain forms include "Blowin' in the Wind" [D], "Signed, Sealed, Delivered" [F], "The Sound of Silence" [Amin], "Still Crazy After All These Years" [C], "She's Always a Woman to Me" [Eb], "I Feel Fine" [F], "Just the Way You Are" [D], "It's Still Rock 'n' Roll to Me" [C], and many others.

A good example of a verse/refrain structure using a cadence is "Signed, Sealed, Delivered." It's simply a repetitive progression with a title set to a cadence.

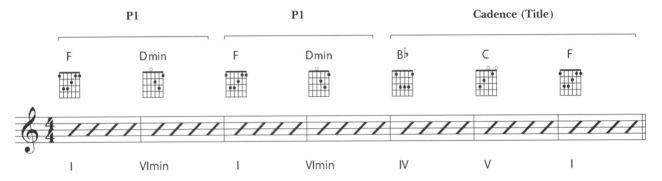

Another way to hear this is that it starts home, on the tonic, then goes away for a while, and finally returns home to the tonic, via a cadence.

Home → Away → Home

Listen

Listen to the next example, which uses the blues progression "I7(♯9) IV7" and the mixed cadence "♭VI V I" from minor to set the title. Notice how the cadence, using new chords, helps the title to stand out.

Listen again, and play along with the recording. The melody also emphasizes the title by using unique notes, ending on the tonic note, and ending on the downbeat.

Writing Exercises

Complete at least one of these exercises. Play and practice it along with one of the drum tracks, or create your own rhythm groove. Use any of the rhythmic tools from unit I to generate your grooves.

■ Practice

Create a song section by repeating a progression a number of times and adding a cadence to the end. Use any progression in any key color.

■ Rewrite the Hits

Choose a verse/refrain from any song you know (or one mentioned in this lesson). First, replace the original ending cadence with one of your own creation. Then, replace the beginning progression(s).

■ Create Your Own Melody

Complete "Practice" above. Then create your own melody over this progression. Emphasize your title by using some of the melodic tools described in this lesson.

■ Write a Song

Complete "Create Your Own Melody" above, and add lyrics. After creating a verse/refrain, create a contrasting bridge.

LESSON 45
Verse: Home/Away

In a verse, you can use cadences to build intensity *and* lead smoothly into a chorus.

Hit songs that use verse cadences to lead into choruses include "The Wind Beneath My Wings" [G], "Night Shift" [G], "Like a Rolling Stone" [C], and many others.

The verse to "The Wind Beneath My Wings" is a repeated progression that builds up to the V chord, which is the most "away" chord in the key. This builds intensity, and it's a great way to set up the coming chorus.

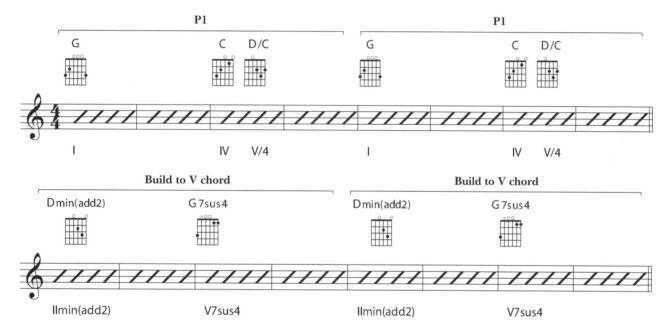

Ending on V is another useful tool when building sections: start on the I chord, go away for a while, and then end on the V chord. Another way to hear this is that it starts home, on the tonic, then goes away:

Home → Away

Listen

Listen to this verse. Notice its harmonic structure, and how the home/away feeling directs the listener's attention to the chorus.

■ "I VImin" repeats

■ "IV V" builds from the major scale color, with the IImin and ♭VII chords added

■ V ending leads nicely into a chorus

Listen again, and play along with the recording. By hanging on the V chord at the end of the verse, the song builds even more intensity. This is *one of the great ways to build excitement in your song: Hang on the V chord.*

Writing Exercises

Complete at least one of these exercises. Play and practice it along with one of the drum tracks, or create your own rhythm groove. Use any of the rhythmic tools from unit I to generate your grooves.

■ Practice

Create a song section by repeating a progression a number of times. Build up to the V chord to the end.

■ Rewrite the Hits

Choose a verse/refrain from any song you know (or one mentioned in this lesson). First, replace the original progression with one of your own creation. Then, replace the build on the V chord with your own variation.

■ Create Your Own Melody

Complete "Practice" above, and create your own melody over it.

■ Write a Song

Complete "Create Your Own Melody" above, and add lyrics. After creating a verse, create a contrasting chorus.

Keys for Exercises 45 to 47

Use the same keys for exercises 45 to 47. You will be combining these song sections together, to form complete songs.

LESSON 46
Building a Chorus with a Cadence

You can use cadences to emphasize a title within a variety of chorus types.

Hit songs with cadences in the chorus include "The Wind Beneath My Wings" [G], "Everybody Plays the Fool" [B♭], "Easy Lover" [Fmin], "How Sweet It Is" [G], "Rock and Roll Hoochie Koo" [Amin], "Time After Time" [C], "Material Girl" [C], "I Can't Stand Losin' You" [Cmin], and many others.

We have seen how to use cadences to emphasize titles in verse/refrain structures. You can also use cadences to emphasize the title in a chorus.

Choruses can be built by using a cadence for every line, or by using a cadence only to set the title and another progression to set non-title lines.

1. Just a Cadence

To create a chorus out of a cadence, simply repeat the cadence, and set all the lyric lines across it. This can be for a variety of different chorus types. After each chorus below, the structure is shown, with the title line indicated by T, and a non-title line by (–).

a. "How Sweet It Is" (T T)

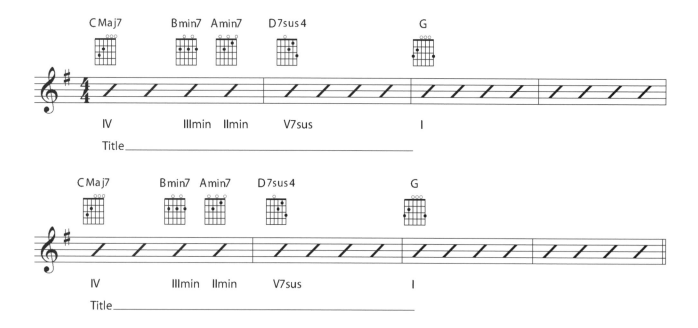

b. "Everybody Plays the Fool" (T – – T)

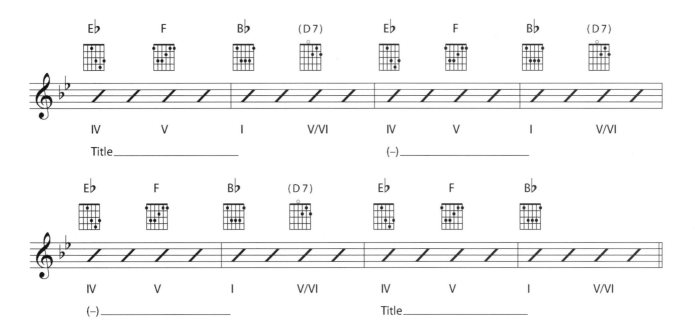

c. "Rock and Roll Hoochie Koo" (T – T –)

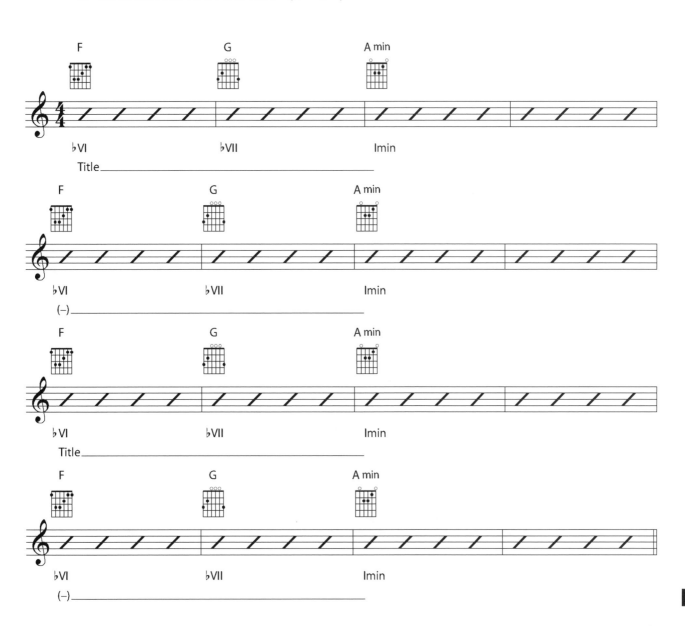

d. "Can't Stand Losin' You"

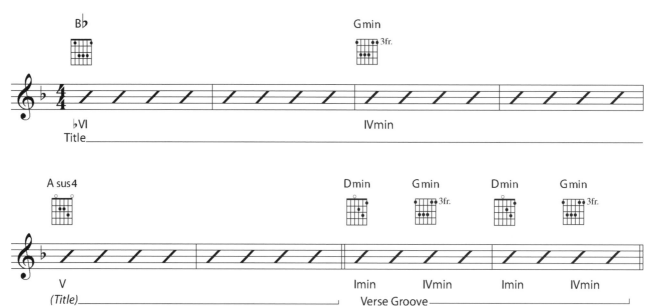

2. Cadence on the Title Only

In many choruses, only the title is set to a cadence. The non-title lines (–) are set to another progression. Notice that these chorus types, beginning on a non-title line, *also avoid the tonic chord until the title.* This also helps the title stand out.

Hit songs with just the title line in a chorus set to a cadence include:

a. "Wind Beneath My Wings" (– – – T)

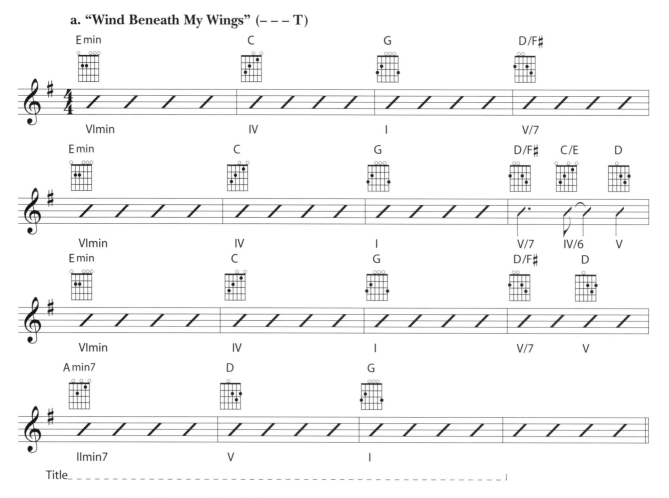

b. "Time After Time" (–T–T)

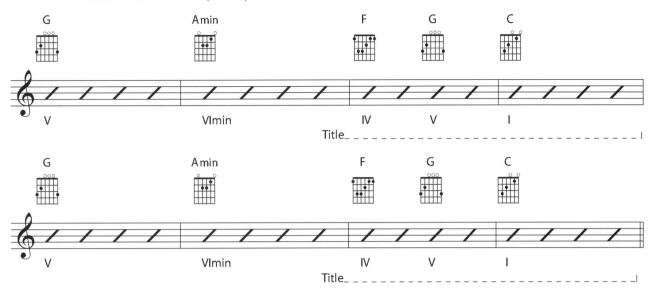

Title␣ _ |

Title␣ _ |

Listen

Listen to the next two chorus examples. The first chorus uses the "VImin V I" major-key cadence and the T T chorus type.

Just a Cadence

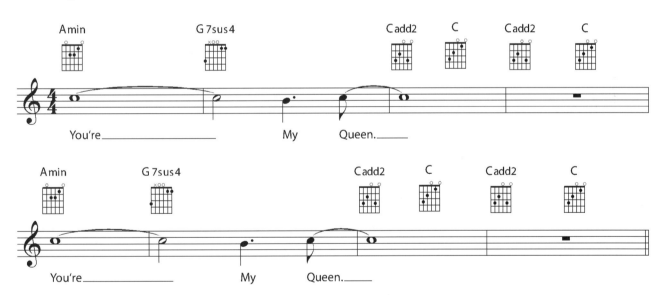

The second chorus uses a mixed plagal cadence "IV IVmin I" to set only the title line in the chorus type – T – T.

Cadence on the Title

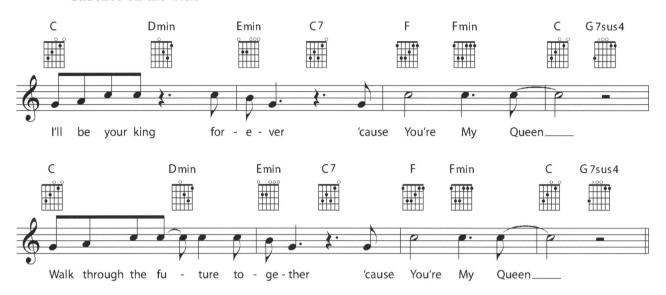

Listen again, and play along with the recording. Notice that the title lines are also emphasized by melodic tools, such as ending on the tonic note (C), long notes, and a downbeat ending.

Writing Exercises

Complete at least one of these exercises. Play and practice it along with one of the drum tracks, or create your own rhythm groove. Use any of the rhythmic tools from unit I to generate your grooves. If you need lyrics, use the lyrics used in this lesson.

Special Note: Create your chorus for this lesson in the same key as the verse from lesson 45, in preparation for lesson 48, "Connecting Sections with Cadences."

■ Practice

1. Create a chorus by repeating a cadence (in any key color). Use any of the chorus types described above under "Just a Cadence."

2. Create a chorus type – T – T. It should begin on the I chord and alternate a cadence with another progression. Set the title to a cadence that reflects the emotion of the title.

■ Rewrite the Hits

Choose a chorus from any song you know (or one mentioned in this lesson). Set the title to an original cadence. Set any non-title lines to a different progression.

■ Create Your Own Melody

Complete "Practice" or "Rewrite the Hits" above. Then create your own melody over this section. Emphasize your title by using some of the melodic tools described in this lesson.

■ Write a Song

Complete "Create Your Own Melody" above, and add lyrics. After creating a chorus, create a contrasting verse.

Keys for Exercises 45 to 47

Use the same keys for exercises 45 to 47. You will be combining these song sections together, to form complete songs.

LESSON 47
Building a Bridge: Away/Away

Using this concept of "home and away" in bridges can help you build intensity. The most harmonically intense bridges both start and end away from home.

Hit songs using "away/away" bridges include "Ticket to Ride" [A], "Help Me Make It through the Night" [C], "Fire" [C], and many others.

A good example of an away/away bridge is "Ticket to Ride." Notice that it begins away from the I chord, on the IV chord, and then moves even further away, to the V chord. This sets up a lot of tension, which eventually resolves in the next section. Also notice that this bridge uses the IV7 blues chord in the major key. This adds additional harmonic tension.

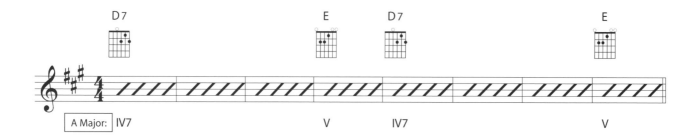

You can also describe it like this:

Away → Away

Listen

Listen to the next bridge. Notice that it uses the progression "IImin IIImin IV," though it is varied in two ways from the most common form:

1. Seventh chords are added to the original chord colors, giving a bluesy effect.

2. The V chord is added to the end.

Listen again, and play along with the recording. Notice that the bridge builds even more intensity by hanging on the V chord, at the end.

Writing Exercises

Complete at least one of these exercises. Play and practice it along with one of the drum tracks, or create your own rhythm groove. Use any of the rhythmic tools from unit I to generate your grooves.

Special Note: Create your bridge for this lesson in the same key as the verse and chorus from lessons 45 and 46, in preparation for lesson 48, "Connecting Sections with Cadences."

■ Practice

Create a bridge by starting on any chord but the I chord. End on the V chord, and hang onto it to build even more intensity.

■ Rewrite the Hits

Choose a bridge from a song you know (or one mentioned in this lesson). First, replace the original progression with one of your own creation. Then, end on the V chord to build intensity.

■ Create Your Own Melody

Complete "Practice" or "Rewrite the Hits" above. Then create your own melody for this bridge.

■ Write a Song

Complete "Create Your Own Melody" above, and add lyrics. After creating a bridge, create a contrasting verse and chorus in the same key.

Keys for Exercises 45 to 47

Use the same keys for exercises 45 to 47. You will be combining these song sections together, to form complete songs.

LESSON 48
Connecting Sections with Cadences

You can also use cadences to connect sections. These connections can reinforce the listeners' expectations or progress in a more surprising way.

There are two ways to connect the verse and chorus by using a cadence: via full cadences or deceptive cadences.

Listen

Full Cadence

Listen to this verse/chorus, which is an example of a verse connecting to a chorus by using a full cadence. Then listen again, and play along with the recording. The V chord, at the end of the verse, goes where you expect it: to the I chord at the beginning of the chorus. This is a common way to connect the verse with the chorus. The verse ends on V, and the chorus begins on I.

LESSON 48 Connecting Sections with Cadences

Deceptive Cadence

Listen to this verse/chorus, where a *deceptive* cadence connects the verse to the chorus. Listen again, and play along with the recording. Here, the V chord at the end of the verse moves deceptively to the VImin chord at the beginning of the chorus. This is a way to surprise your listeners: Begin the chorus with a chord other than I.

Listen to this verse/chorus/bridge. What kinds of cadences are used?

Listen again, and play along with the recording. Notice how smoothly all the sections connect:

1. The verse builds intensity and connects to the chorus by using the V chord.

2. The V chord moves deceptively to the VImin chord at the chorus beginning.

3. The bridge also builds intensity; it will connect to the next chorus by using the V chord as well.

Also notice some ways the sections contrast:

1. Each section begins on a different chord.

2. Each section has a new chord (or more than one new chord).

3. A full cadence appears only in the chorus.

4. Each section has a different phrase length.

How is each section contrasted melodically? What are the emotional high points of the song? How are these high points brought out harmonically? Melodically?

Writing Exercises

■ All Levels

Combine the verse you created in lesson 45 with each chorus you created in 46. Notice the effect of the different choruses following the same verse. Choose the one that works best. You've created a verse/chorus song!

Try each verse/chorus combination with the bridge you created in lesson 47. Choose the best combination, and you've created a verse/chorus song with a bridge!

Play and practice it along with one of the drum tracks, or create your own rhythm groove. Use any of the rhythmic tools from unit I to generate your grooves.

UNIT IX
Modulation

Modulation is an extension of the home/away idea. A modulation takes your song *far* away from the tonic chord. In fact, it takes it far away from the tonic *key*, into a whole new *key*. It is like moving home from one place to another. In this unit, you'll learn some common types of modulation to a new key. This is a great way to surprise your listeners, keep your songs sounding fresh, and create the impression of arriving at a new place.

A. Ways of Changing Keys

There are three common ways of changing keys. In this part, you'll learn the most common target keys used for modulation, and some easy ways to get to those keys.

LESSON 49
Parallel-Key Modulation

A *parallel-key* modulation is one that changes the key color, but maintains the same tonic note. This is the simplest form of modulation, but it can be very effective, especially for reflecting significant new directions in the lyric story.

Hit songs using parallel-key modulations include "I'll Be Back" [Amin to A], "I'm Alright" [D Mixolydian to D Dorian], "Foxy Lady" [F♯ Dorian to F♯ blues], "Here, There, and Everywhere" [Gmin to G], "While My Guitar Gently Weeps" [Amin to A], and many others.

Parallel keys are different key colors based on the same tonic note. The following pairs are parallel keys:

- A major and A minor

- F Mixolydian and F minor

- D Dorian and D major

To create a parallel modulation, follow a chord progression in the first key with a new progression in a parallel key of a different color.

Listen

 Listen to this progression. Notice that the G Mixolydian progression modulates to G Dorian.

G Mixolydian

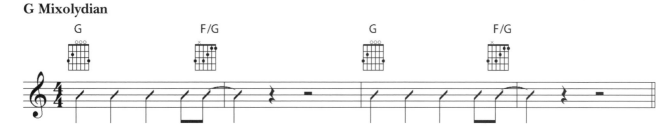

G Dorian

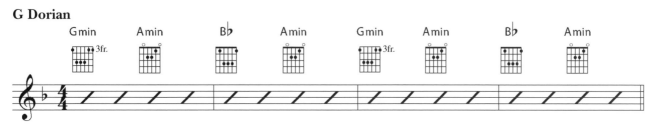

Listen again, and play along with the recording. Notice that the new key color has a very different emotional tone than the first one. *This harmonic change should reflect a change in the lyric story.*

Writing Exercises

Complete at least one of these exercises. Play and practice it along with one of the drum tracks, or create your own rhythm groove. Use any of the rhythmic tools from unit I to generate your grooves.

■ Practice

Create an original variation on a chord progression in any key color. Follow it with another progression in a different key color *on the same tonic note.*

■ Rewrite the Hits

Choose a progression from any song you know (or one mentioned in this lesson). Follow it with a progression from a song in a different key color, *but based on the same tonic.*

■ Create Your Own Melody

Complete either "Practice" or "Rewrite the Hits." Then compose a melody that spans both key color regions. Reflect the different emotion of the new key.

■ Write a Song

Complete the "Create Your Own Melody" exercise above, and add lyrics that reflect the two different keys.

LESSON 50
Relative-Key Modulation

Relative keys are keys that have the same notes and chords. A *relative-key* modulation moves between two relative keys. It is based on the idea of the deceptive cadence. This type of modulation is an easy and effective way to surprise your listener. Since the new key often has a new color, it also often reflects a new lyric idea.

Hit songs using relative-key modulations include "We Can Work It Out" [D to Bmin], "Could You Be Love" [Bmin to D], "King of Pain" [Bmin to D], and many others.

The deceptive cadence is where the V chord goes somewhere surprising, instead of to the I chord. The relative-key modulation is based on that same idea. The only difference is: *you stay in the key of the deceptive chord.*

Relative Keys

Below are the scales and chords of two keys: C major and A minor. Notice that they share the same notes and chords (with the exception of minor's possible V chord, E major). These two keys are therefore called a *relative pair*. The key A minor is the *relative minor* of C major; C major is the *relative major* of A minor.

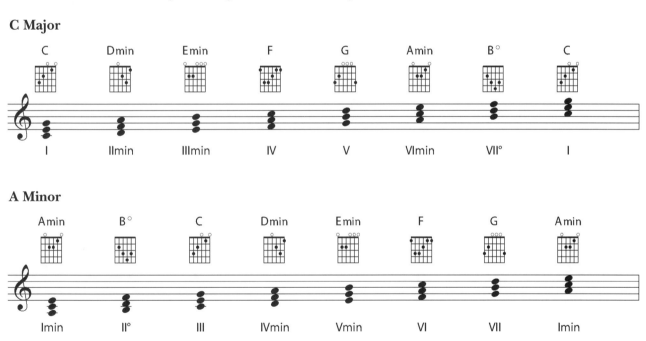

C Major

C	Dmin	Emin	F	G	Amin	B°	C
I	IImin	IIImin	IV	V	VImin	VII°	I

A Minor

Amin	B°	C	Dmin	Emin	F	G	Amin
Imin	II°	III	IVmin	Vmin	VI	VII	Imin

Since relative keys have the same notes and chords, it's easy to modulate between them. Here are the most common types of relative-key modulation.

Modulation 1. Minor to Relative Major

The first type of modulation goes from a minor key to its relative major. To create a smooth modulation, find a chord that is common to cadences in both keys. Approach this chord in the first key, and then leave it in the second key. Because this kind of chord is a turning point, it is called a *pivot chord*.

From your earlier study of cadences, you might remember that the "away chord" in the minor-key full cadence is the ♭VII, and in a major key, the V. In this major/minor relative pair, these chords are the same: G. Therefore, the chord G will be the pivot chord of this modulation. It will act as a door out of A minor, and into C major.

A Minor: ♭VII
C Major: V

If the song is in A minor, the listener will expect the G to cadence to Amin. If you wish to surprise your listeners, rather than to give them what they expect (Amin), modulate instead to C. To do this, end the A minor section of the song on the G chord. Then, cadence to the chord C, the tonic of C major. C becomes the song's new "home," and it should remain in the key of C major.

Listen

Listen to modulation, from minor to relative major. Notice how the G chord in measures 3–4 moves smoothly to the C chord in measure 5. It has changed keys from A minor to C major!

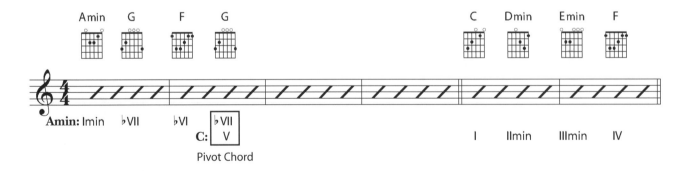

Listen again, and play along with the recording. Notice that the new key (C) is established with a chord progression. This reinforces C as the song's new home key.

Modulation 2. Major to Relative Minor

Modulating to a key's relative *major* is similar to modulating to its relative minor. You just reverse the process. The V chord in major is the ♭VII in the relative minor. Look at it like this:

C Major: V
A Minor: ♭**VII**

This V chord is now your door out of C major and into A minor.

To modulate from major to relative minor, simply end a chord progression on the V chord of the major key, but then resolve it to the VImin chord, which becomes the I minor chord of the new home key, in relative minor.

Listen

Listen to this progression from major to relative minor. Notice how the G chord in measures 3–4 moves smoothly to the A minor chord in measure 5. It has modulated from C to A minor!

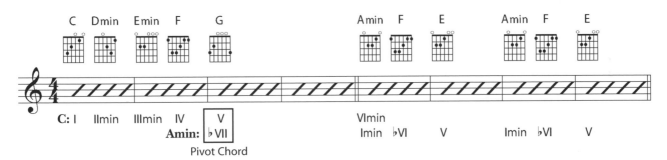

Listen again, and play along with the recording. Again, notice how the new key of A minor is established with a progression.

Writing Exercises

80 to 85

Complete at least one of these exercises. Play and practice it along with one of the drum tracks, or create your own rhythm groove. Use any of the rhythmic tools from unit I to generate your grooves.

■ Practice

1. Create a minor-key chord progression that ends on the ♭VII chord. Modulate to the I chord of the relative major key. Create a major chord progression in this new key.

2. Create a major-key chord progression that ends on the V chord. Modulate to the Imin chord of the relative minor key. Create a minor-key chord progression in this new key.

■ Rewrite the Hits

1. Choose a progression from any minor-key song you know (or one mentioned in this lesson). Vary it to end on the ♭VII chord. Modulate to the I chord of the relative-major key. Create a major-key chord progression in this new key.

2. Choose a progression from any major-key song you know (or one mentioned in this lesson). Vary it to end on the V chord. Modulate to the Imin chord of the relative-minor key. Create a minor-key chord progression in this new key.

■ Create Your Own Melody

Complete either "Practice" or "Rewrite the Hits." Then compose a melody in each key that reflects that key's emotion.

■ Write a Song

1. Create a minor-key verse that modulates to the relative major for the chorus.

2. Create a major-key verse/refrain that modulates to the relative minor for the bridge.

LESSON 51
Surprising-Key Modulation

The *surprising-key* modulation is also based on the idea of the deceptive cadence. The difference is that the new key is a not a relative one. This creates more contrast, and more surprise, and it is a particularly effective way to bring your audience to an unexpected place.

Hit songs that include surprising-key modulations include "Something in the Way She Moves" [C to A], "Bell Bottom Blues" [C to A], "St. Elmo's Fire" [C to A], and many others.

We discussed deceptive cadences going from V to VI, or in they key of C major, a G chord to an A *major* chord. The surprising-key modulation is based on that same idea. The only difference is that you stay *in the key of the deceptive chord*, in this case A major.

Listen

Listen to this progression, which modulates to a surprising key. Notice the buildup on the V chord, and then the deceptive resolution to the A major chord. The song then continues in the key of A. It has changed keys from C major to A major.

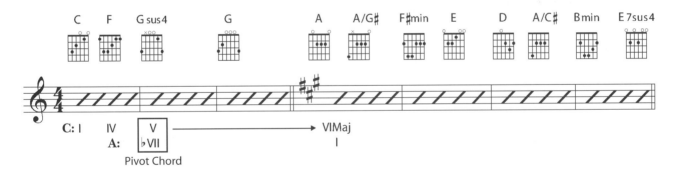

Listen again, and play along with the recording. Again, notice how the new key of A is established with a chord progression. You can use this type of modulation to modulate between many surprising keys, but the most common one is I major to VI major [C to A major].

Writing Exercises

Complete at least one of these exercises. Play and practice it along with one of the drum tracks, or create your own rhythm groove. Use any of the rhythmic tools from unit I to generate your grooves.

■ Practice

Create a major-key progression that ends on the V chord. Resolve it to a surprising chord (e.g., VI major, IV major, etc.). Treat this surprising chord as the I chord of a new key, and create a progression that reinforces it as the new tonic.

■ Rewrite the Hits

Choose a progression from any song you know (or one mentioned in this lesson). Vary it to end on the V chord. Resolve it to a surprising chord (such as VI major, IV major, etc.). Treat this surprising chord as the I chord of a new key, and create a progression that reinforces it as the new tonic.

■ Create Your Own Melody

Complete either "Practice" or "Rewrite the Hits." Compose a melody in each key that reflects the emotion of that key.

■ Write a Song

Create a verse in a major key that modulates to a surprising key for the chorus.

B. Modulation in Songs

In part B, you will use modulation in the context of the song. You can either modulate within a section or modulate to link two different sections together.

LESSON 52
Modulation *Within* a Section

The most common use for a modulation within a song section is to create a two-part verse. Any of the modulation types we discussed can be used within a section.

Hit songs that modulate within a section include "How Can We Be Lovers" [Amin to Cmin], "Here There and Everywhere" [B♭ to Gmin], and many others.

Listen

Listen to this verse that contains a modulation. Notice that this verse begins with a progression in A minor, modulates to the relative key of C major, and then continues in C, ending on the V chord. The V of C will then lead smoothly into the chorus.

Listen again, and play along with the recording. Notice that the lyrics ideas change, similar to the changes in key colors. The verse also builds intensity before the chorus by holding onto the V chord.

Writing Exercises

Complete at least one of these exercises. Play and practice it along with one of the drum tracks, or create your own rhythm groove. Use any of the rhythmic tools from unit I to generate your grooves.

■ Practice

Create a song section by repeating a progression, ending it on a chord you can use for modulation [V in major, ♭VII in minor]. Use any of the modulation types you learned in this unit to modulate to a new key. Create the second part of the verse in that new key.

■ Rewrite the Hits

Choose a progression from any song you know (or one mentioned in this lesson). Vary it to end on a chord you can use for modulation [V in major, ♭VII in minor]. Use any of the modulation types you learned in this unit to modulate to a new key. Choose a different song, and then use it to create the second part of the verse.

■ Create Your Own Melody

Complete "Practice" or "Rewrite the Hits" above. Then create your own melody that reflects the key colors.

■ Write a Song

Complete "Create Your Own Melody" above. After creating a two-part verse, modulate to another key and create a contrasting chorus.

LESSON 53
Modulation *Between* Sections

Modulations are often used to link two song sections—most commonly, a verse and chorus, or going into a bridge. Any of the modulation types can be used to link two song sections.

Hit songs that modulate between sections include "We Can Work It Out" [D Mixolydian to Bmin], "St. Elmo's Fire" [C to A], "King of Pain" [Bmin to D], "Could You Be Love" [Bmin to D], "Something in the Way She Moves" [C to A], "Bell Bottom Blues" [C to A], "While My Guitar Gently Weeps" [Amin to A], and many others.

Listen

Listen to this verse/chorus pair, connected by a modulation. Notice that the verse ends on the V chord in C [G]. As we discussed, the V chord is especially useful in modulations, as it is an easy link to relative keys or to common surprise-keys. In this example, the G chord resolves into the A *major* chord for a surprising modulation into the chorus.

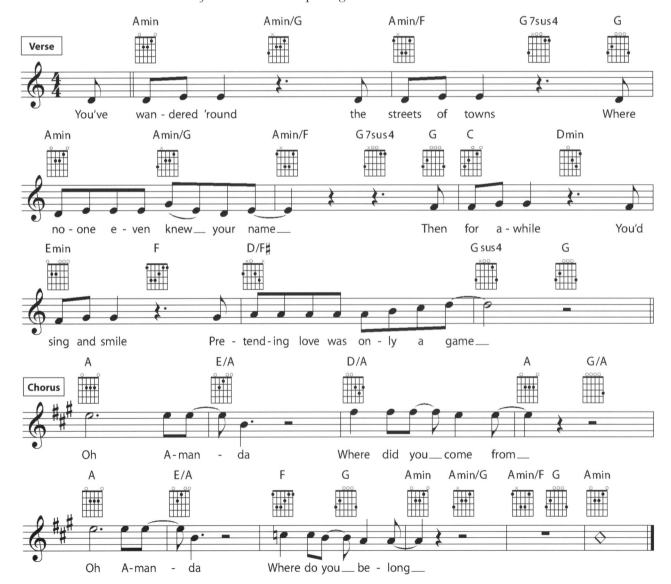

Listen again, and play along with the recording. Notice the way that the surprise-key modulation to the key of A [VI major] gives the song an emotional lift at the chorus. Since the chorus is the emotional high point of the lyric, this type of modulation is especially effective at this point.

How else do the sections contrast harmonically? Melodically?

Writing Exercises

Complete at least one of these exercises. Play and practice it along with one of the drum tracks, or create your own rhythm groove. Use any of the rhythmic tools from unit I to generate your grooves.

■ Practice

Create a verse or verse/refrain that ends on a chord you can use for modulation (V in major, ♭VII in minor). Resolve it deceptively to a surprising key. Create a second section (chorus to follow a verse, or bridge to follow a verse/refrain) in that new key.

■ Rewrite the Hits

Choose a progression from any song you know (or one mentioned in this lesson). Create a verse or verse/refrain that ends on a chord you can use for modulation (V in major, ♭VII in minor). Use any of the modulation types you learned in this unit to modulate to a new key. Create the second section (chorus to follow a verse, or bridge to follow a verse/refrain) using a progression from a different song.

■ Create Your Own Melody

Complete "Practice" or "Rewrite the Hits." Then create your own melody that reflects the different key colors.

■ Write a Song

Complete "Create Your Own Melody," and add lyrics that reflect the different key colors.

APPENDIX

These charts show the seven chords of each key color in all twelve possible transpositions. Use them to transpose power progressions or any other chord progressions you wish to use.

■ Find the key names by reading down the left margin [C, D-flat, D, E-flat etc.].

■ Potential added notes are shown in parentheses at the top of each column.

■ Read across each line to find the seven chords in that key. For example, the chords of G major are:

G	Amin	Bmin	C	D	Emin	F♯°
I	IImin	IIImin	IV	V	VImin	VII°

Major Keys

Minor Keys

Remember the optional major V chord, which is listed in parentheses in the last column of each key.

Optional
V chord

Imin7 II°(min7♭5) ♭III(Maj7) IVmin(7) V(min7)   ♭VI(Maj7)   ♭VII(7)   Imin7   V(7)

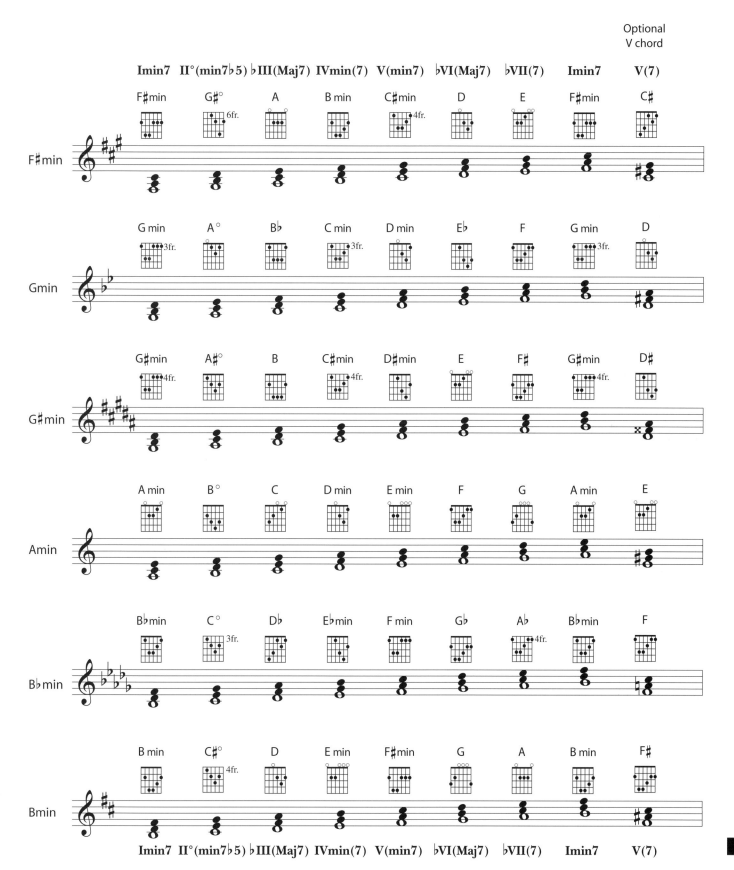

Mixolydian Keys

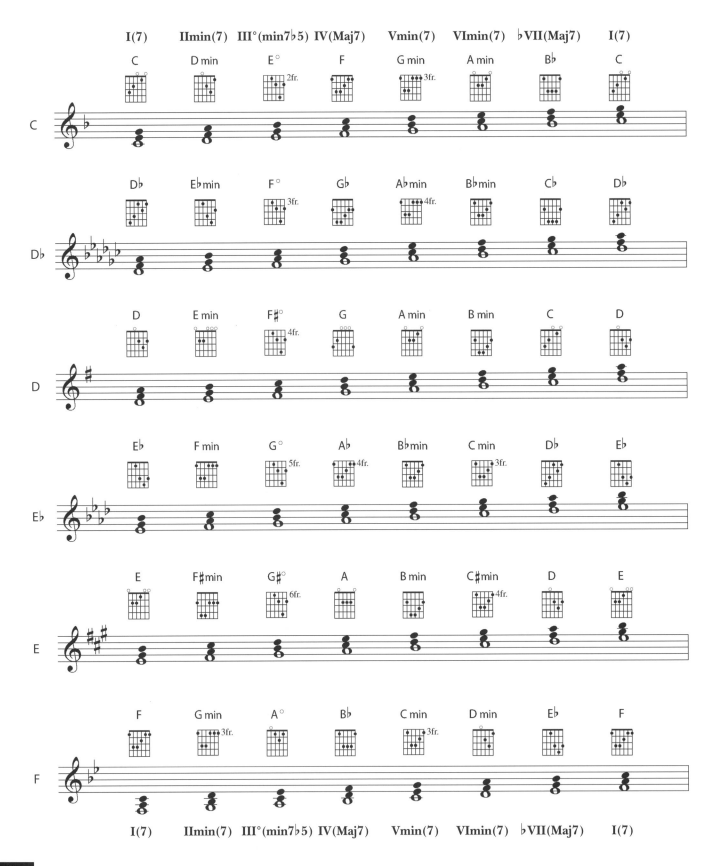

Dorian Keys

Blues Keys

What's Next?

Thank you for reading *The Songwriter's Workshop: Harmony*. I hope that these tools help you write some great songs.

Now that you've completed this book, your next step is to incorporate these new skills into your everyday songwriting. In the same way that instrumentalists practice scales, you should also warm up before you write. Here are some ideas for daily songwriting exercises:

- Create six chord progressions under the same melody.

- Create six grooves of the same progression.

Continue using this book as a source of ideas. Go back and do some different writing exercises. You will be amazed at how much easier the tools become after you've already used them.

Also, try the other products in *The Songwriter's Workshop* series: the book on melody and the various online songwriting classes at Berkleemusic.com. These materials are filled with similar tools that will help you create and develop ideas. They are all based on how hit songs really are created, and I hope that you find them as useful as I do. The online classes give you the opportunity to participate in a community of songwriters, guided by a Berklee songwriting professor (maybe me!).

Sing, study, and learn from the great songwriters of the past. And keep writing.

Jimmy Kachulis
Professor
Berklee College of Music

About the Author

Jimmy Kachulis has trained thousands of songwriters, including Grammy-winning artists on Rounder, A&M, and MCA; staff writers at Almo Irving, Sony, Warner Brothers, and EMI; A&R people at Warner Brothers, BMG, and Sony; artists on independent labels; as well as independent songwriters. He currently teaches songwriting and lyric writing at Berklee College of Music and conducts songwriting clinics nationwide. Jimmy's songs have been recorded and broadcast internationally on *The Sopranos, Touched by an Angel, Jag, All My Children, The Young and the Restless, One Life to Live, The Jamie Foxx Show, Movie of the Week,* and various Showtime movies. He has written for Eric Gale, Stuff, and Martha Reeves. He has a BS from Hunter College CUNY and an MA in Ethnomusicology from Tufts University.

Jimmy has authored the *Songwriter's Workshop* series and *Essential Songwriter* for Berklee Press. In addition, he has created three online courses for Berkleemusic.com in *The Songwriter's Workshop* series: Harmony, Melody, and Hit Song Forms. For more information about Jimmy Kachulis, his books, and his music, see www.jimmykachulis.com.